Kingston ...

on Libraries

returned
...

EXCEL MASTER

Max Begley

Letts Educational
Chiswick Centre
414 Chiswick High Road
London W4 5TF
Tel: 020 8996 3333
Fax: 020 8996 8390

First published 2004

Commissioned by Cassandra Birmingham

Editorial, cover and inside design and project
management by DP Press Ltd., Kent.

British Library Cataloguing in Publication
Data. A CIP record of this book is available
from the British Library.

ISBN 1843153297

Letts Educational is a division of Granada
Learning, part of Granada plc.

Acknowledgements
The author and publisher are grateful to the
copyright holders for permission to use quoted
materials and images.
Screen shots reprinted by permission from
Microsoft Corporation.
Every effort has been made to obtain
permission for the use of copyright material.
The author and publisher will gladly receive
information enabling them to rectify any error
or omission in subsequent editions.

Printed in Italy

CONTENTS

SKILLS

.: Spreadsheets :.

A spreadsheet is really just a normal page divided into thousands of little bits. Each bit has a name, which helps you find it on the page. We will see how this can help us do our work in later chapters. Each bit or cell on the spreadsheet is given a name or **cell address**. This is done in a logical way, much like a map. Cells in a vertical line are called a **column** and these are given a letter. Cells in a horizontal line are called a **row** and are given a number. So the cell at the top left of the spreadsheet has the address A1.

Microsoft Excel - Book1

File Edit View Insert Format Tools Data Window Help

A1

	A	B	C	D	E	F	G	H
1								
2								
3								
4								
5								
6								
7								
8								
9								
10								
11								
12								
13								
14								
15								
16								

.: Entering data in a spreadsheet cell :.

To enter data in to a cell, simply position the cursor (a small white cross) on the cell where you want your data, click the mouse and type the required information. We will look at changing the look of the data later. Before you start entering data on to your spreadsheet, it is a good idea to have a plan of how you are going to set everything out.

 PC MASTER TIP

If you have trouble imagining how you will set things out, why not draw a quick sketch with a pen and paper? Do not worry if things go wrong the first time!

SKILL IN ACTION

Harry the Hotelier uses spreadsheets to keep track of all the money in his hotel. By placing all the bookings on to a spreadsheet, he can see how much money is coming in. He can also check this against the amount of money that is going out of the hotel when he pays his staff and buys food for the restaurant.

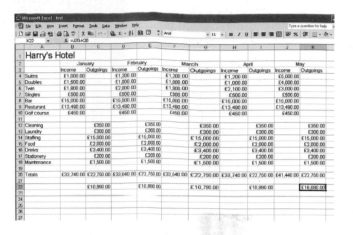

It is important for Harry to have a good layout for his spreadsheet so he can see each month clearly. He has to enter data each month to keep the spreadsheet up-to-date.

Harry can add data throughout the year and then compare what is happening from month to month. This is very useful for finding out which are the best months for making money at the hotel.

EXERCISE

Can you identify each cell and enter data in some of them?

0100101010110100101001011101001010101110101011011100001010110

SKILLS

.: Cell address :.

Open a spreadsheet and click the mouse on any cell. You will see that the column and row labels that the cell is in are highlighted. The cell address is also shown at the top left of the screen in what is called the 'name box'.

.: Entering data :.

Once you have decided where you want your data, click on the cell and type the word or number. To move to a different cell, use either the cursor keys or the mouse. If you press the **Enter** key once you have finished typing, the next cell will automatically be selected. This is very useful when you are typing a lot of items in a column or row.

Microsoft Excel - Book1

File   Edit   View   Insert   Format   T

B4   fx

	A	B	C
1			
2			
3			
4			
5			
6			
7			
8			
9			
10			
11			

PC MASTER TIP

Always plan the layout before you start inputting the data.

1001001010110100101001011101001010101110101011011100001010

 PROGRESS CHECK EXERCISE

Can you identify a cell?

Using the mouse, click on any cell on the spreadsheet. Check the cell address in the 'name box' in the top left-hand corner.

Can you type in a list of items?

You can type a list very simply by starting in a cell and using the **return** key (Enter) at the end of each word.

If you make a mistake, how do you correct it?

There are two ways of doing this. Firstly, if you are still entering data, use the **backspace** key to delete the data. If the whole cell is wrong, then click in the cell and press the **delete** key.

Microsoft Excel - Book1

File Edit View Insert Format

A11

	A	B	C
1			
2	suitcase		
3	towel		
4	shirts		
5	shorts		
6	belt		
7	sandals		
8	trousers		
9	sunblock		
10	hat		
11			
12			
13			

 MASTERCLASS

Can you set up a timetable for your week?

HINT: This is a simple table. Place the days of the week in cells B1 to H1 and the hours of the day in column A.

Microsoft Excel - Book1

File Edit View Insert Format Tools Data Window

B4

	A	B	C	D	E	Fri
1		Monday	Tuesday	Wednesda	Thursday	
2	8.00am					
3	9.00am					
4	10.00am					
5	11.00am					
6	12.00am					
7	1.00pm					
8	2.00pm					
9	3.00pm					
10	4.00pm					
11	5.00pm					
12	6.00pm					
13	7.00pm					
14	8.00pm					
15	9.00pm					
16	10.00pm					
17	11.00pm					

SKILLS

.: Saving in Excel :.

A spreadsheet is often better than using pen, paper and a calculator as you are able to save your work so that you can come back to it and adapt it later.

When saving your work, you will need to think of a suitable name and be sure that you know where you are saving it.

Your work will be saved as a **file**. It is best to put the file into a **folder** with similar files so that you can find it again easily. On most computers, these folders will be located in the **My Documents** folder. The first time you save a file, you should give it a name. Once you have saved the work you can resave it using the same name.

.: Choosing a file name :.

When saving a spreadsheet, you should also consider whether you are going to update the sheet and need to keep a copy of the first one you saved. If so, it is often useful to choose a file name that you can add to, e.g. 'May 2004'. That way your next one can be saved as 'June 2004' etc.

If you have saved the work, you need to know how to open it when you need it again.

PC MASTER TIP

Get into the habit of giving your files logical names so that it is easy to find them in the future.

SKILL IN ACTION

In her job, Sandy the Secretary has hundreds of files to keep. Some of these she does not use again so she deletes them. Others she keeps as a reference. Some she updates every day. It is very important that she keeps the correct ones, so Sandy uses a filing system that is very similar to keeping files in a filing cabinet.

Sandy keeps the files she uses every day in a folder called 'Daily updates'. Each day she knows exactly where the files are and which ones need updating.

When Sandy saves the updated files, she saves them into a new folder and gives it that day's date. If she needs to open those files again later, she simply finds the folder with the date she wants and opens them.

EXERCISE

Save a file called '5th March' then save the same spreadsheet as '6th March'.

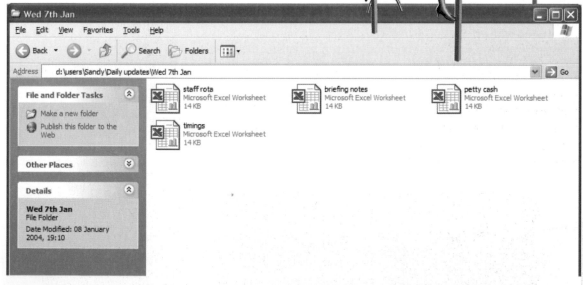

`01001010110100101001011101001010101011101010110111000010101101`

SKILLS

.: Saving your work :.

To save your work for the first time, you will need to check that it has a sensible name. The computer will guess that you want to call it 'Book 1' (or something similar). This is usually not appropriate as you want to call it something that will remind you of the image. You need to use the **Save As** function. Click on **File** then **Save As**, as shown below.

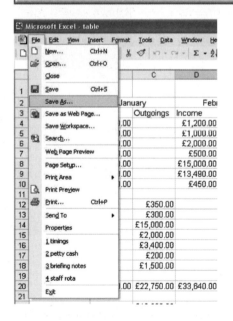

.: Naming your work :.

Write an appropriate file name in and check the file is in the correct folder. Finally, click **OK** to save your work.

.: Opening your work :.

There are two ways to open your work. If you find the file in a folder, you can double click on the file. The computer will try to guess which program you want to use. You can usually see this by the icon next to the file name. If this does not work, open the required application first, then click on the **Open** button, or click on **File** then **Open**. You should then be able to locate the file and open it.

.: Using Save As :.

If you want to save the file after opening it, unless you want to rename the file, you can just use the **Save** button. If you want to give it a new file name, change the file name by saving the spreadsheet using **Save As**.

PC MASTER TIP

Sometimes you may want to save a spreadsheet for a different application. You need to save it as a *.**csv** file.

110100101011010010100101110100101010101110101011011100001010

 ## PROGRESS CHECK EXERCISE

Can you save a file with the same name as another file?

If you need the same name for two files, you will need to change the name of the second file slightly, for example 'sheet1' and 'sheet2'.

Can you change the name of a file once you have named it?

Open the folder containing the file and right click the mouse on the **file** icon. Then go to **Rename** and change the name of your file.

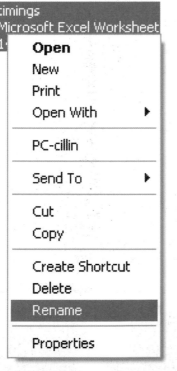

Can you save a document in a new folder?

Save a spreadsheet in a folder called 'Homework'. Click on one of the icons that appears at the top of the **Save As** box.

Now write in the name 'School work'. You can open this folder to save the work in.

 ## MASTERCLASS

Can you save a document as a *.csv file? You need to change the file type when you save it.

SKILLS

.: Print preview :.

Many documents that you create will need printing. Spreadsheets need to be printed carefully. Often you need to set the page up so that it prints out without wasting lots of paper.

To see what your work looks like, click on the **print preview** icon in the toolbar.

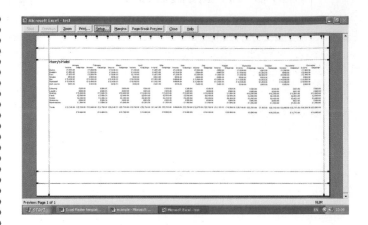

Print preview icon   Print icon

.: Print preview :.

Another screen will now show you what your work would look like if it were printed out.

.: Page setup :.

If your work is fairly small, it usually fits on one page easily. Sometimes you may have to alter the orientation of the page to fit your work on one page. You can do this in the **Page Setup** menu.

.: Printing :.

To print your work once it has been set up, there are two main methods. You can use the **File** menu or you can click the **print** icon on the toolbar.

PC MASTER TIP

In the **Page Setup** window you can automatically fit your spreadsheet to your page by choosing the **Fit to:** option in the scaling section.

SKILL IN ACTION

Each year, Harry the Hotelier has to show his accounts to the Inland Revenue. He prints out a copy of each month's takings so that they are easy to read.

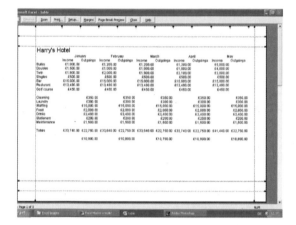

Sometimes Harry can fit all the data on one page. However, a whole year's data fits better on two pages.

Harry also prints out his staff wage slips each month. This is so both he and each of his staff can have a copy of their monthly earnings. Harry keeps a record of the pay slips on his computer so he can refer back to them if he needs to.

EXERCISE

Press the **print preview** icon on your spreadsheet. Can you read your spreadsheet as it is?

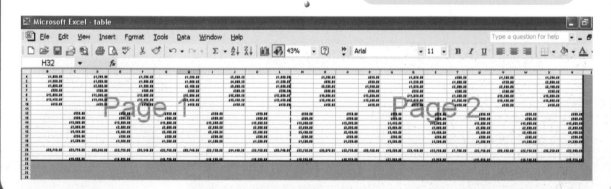

SKILLS

.: Print preview :.

Some people find printing from a spreadsheet hard and make lots of mistakes. However if you follow a few simple rules you cannot go wrong.

The first step is to see what your work looks like by either clicking on the **print preview** icon or by selecting **Print Preview** from the **File** menu.

.: Print preview checks :.

Now do the following checks:

1. How many pages does my work fill?
2. Can I get the whole spreadsheet on one page?
3. Do I need to change the orientation?

If your work looks fine, you can go ahead and press the **print** icon.

.: Page orientation :.

If your work is too large for one page, you can change a few things to help it fit. Try changing the orientation. This means changing the page from portrait view to landscape view.

 Landscape

.: 'Fit to:' option :.

If changing the page orientation does not work, there is another way of getting it on one page. In the **Page Setup** window choose the **Fit to:** option and make sure it has one page selected. This will shrink your work to fit on to one page. Make sure it is big enough to read!

Scaling

Adjust to: `79` % normal size

Fit to: `2` page(s) wide by

💡 PC MASTER TIP

To get back to the normal spreadsheet view from the print preview view, you must click on the **close** button in the top toolbar.

PROGRESS CHECK EXERCISE

Can you change the orientation of the page?

Select **Page Setup** then check the landscape option.

Can you adjust the size of the spreadsheet to fit on one or more pages?

Use the **Page Setup** window with the **Fit to:** option to enlarge or shrink your work.

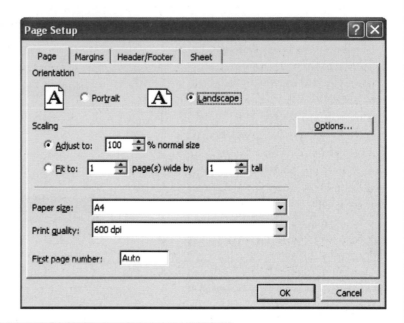

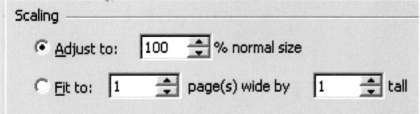

 ## MASTERCLASS

There is another way of changing the size of your work. Use the **Adjust to:** option from the **Page Setup** window. Increase the size of a small spreadsheet to fit the whole of one side of A4.

SKILLS

.: Styling text :.

Often it is much easier to understand a spreadsheet if it is laid out well and the important parts are highlighted. There are several ways of doing this.

There are two drop down menus in the top menu bar that enable a change of style and size of the text. This is the most common method of changing the standard format.

.: Using colour :.

Changing the colour of the text or the background of the cell helps link cells with common pieces of data together.

.: Colours and styles :.

A combination of different text sizes, styles and colours can make a complex spreadsheet easy to read and understand.

Microsoft Excel - Book2

	A	B	C	D	E	F	G	H
1								
2		Monday	Tuesday	Wednesday	Thursday	Friday	Saturday	Sunday
3								
4								
5								
6								
7								
8								

Microsoft Excel - table

	A	B	C	D	E	F	G
1		W	L	D	Played	Points	Rank
2	Leicester	4	6	0	10	12	6
3	Wasps	4	6	0	10	12	6
4	Harlequins	3	7	0	10	9	8
5	Sale	2	8	0	10	6	9
6	Saracens	4	5	1	10	13	5
7	Bath	8	0	2	10	26	1
8	Northampton	5	3	2	10	17	3
9	Gloucester	4	4	2	10	14	4
10	Newcastle	6	1	3	10	21	2
11							
12							
13	Win	3					
14	Lose	0					
15	Draw	1					
16	Bonus (>4 tries)	1					
17							
18							
19							
20							

PC MASTER TIP

Too many colours can have the opposite effect. It is best to use only a couple of colours and fonts that go well together.

10010010101011010010100101011101001010101011010101011011100001010

 ## SKILL IN ACTION

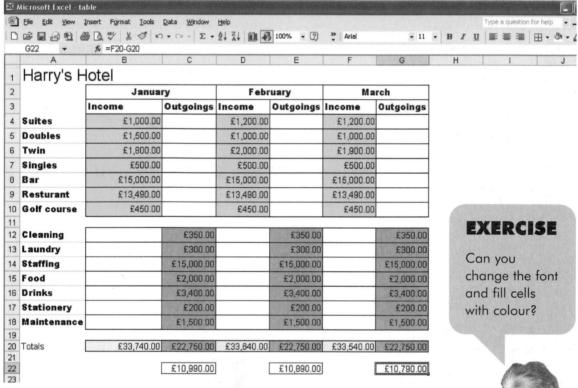

Microsoft Excel - table									
	January		February		March				
	Income	Outgoings	Income	Outgoings	Income	Outgoings			
Suites	£1,000.00		£1,200.00		£1,200.00				
Doubles	£1,500.00		£1,000.00		£1,000.00				
Twin	£1,800.00		£2,000.00		£1,900.00				
Singles	£500.00		£500.00		£500.00				
Bar	£15,000.00		£15,000.00		£15,000.00				
Resturant	£13,490.00		£13,490.00		£13,490.00				
Golf course	£450.00		£450.00		£450.00				
Cleaning		£350.00		£350.00		£350.00			
Laundry		£300.00		£300.00		£300.00			
Staffing		£15,000.00		£15,000.00		£15,000.00			
Food		£2,000.00		£2,000.00		£2,000.00			
Drinks		£3,400.00		£3,400.00		£3,400.00			
Stationery		£200.00		£200.00		£200.00			
Maintenance		£1,500.00		£1,500.00		£1,500.00			
Totals	£33,740.00	£22,750.00	£33,840.00	£22,750.00	£33,540.00	£22,750.00			
		£10,990.00		£10,890.00		£10,790.00			

EXERCISE

Can you change the font and fill cells with colour?

Sandy the Secretary works in Harry's hotel. She often produces spreadsheets for him. To make each one easy to understand, Sandy changes the way that the text looks on the spreadsheet. She tries to follow a standard pattern so that the colours are the same each time she produces a spreadsheet.

She makes the titles bold and enlarges the font to size 14. She shades Income cells light green and makes the Outgoings cells purple.

SKILLS

.: Changing the font :.

To change the look of the text, you can do several things. You can change the type and size of the font, and colour the text or the cell, or both.

To change the font, select the cells that require changing with the mouse. Then click on the down arrow next to the **font** button on the toolbar. Select the font that you require and it will change.

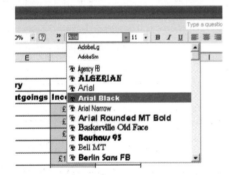

.: Changing the font size :.

Changing the font size is very similar. Choose the size of font required from the drop down menu and the selected text will automatically change.

.: Changing the font colour :.

To change the font colour, select the cells that require changing with the mouse. Then click on the down arrow next to the **font colour** icon on the toolbar. Select the colour that you require and it will change.

Font colour icon

.: Changing the cell colour :.

Changing the cell colour is similar. Choose a colour from the drop down menu and the selected cell will automatically change.

 PC MASTER TIP

The data in a column is often very narrow but the label for the column is much wider. Instead of creating unnecessarily wide columns or shortening the labels, you can rotate the text and apply borders that are rotated to the same degree as the text by clicking on **Format**, then **Cells**.

PROGRESS CHECK EXERCISE

Can you change the size and type of the data in any cell?

Can you change the colour of the font and the background of the cell?

Can you choose suitable colours that look good and will show the text clearly, even when printed out in black and white?

Microsoft Excel - table

File Edit View Insert Format Tools Data Window Help

Arial   11

Harry's Hotel

	January		February		March	
	Income	Outgoings	Income	Outgoings	Income	Outgoings
Suites	£1,000.00		£1,200.00		£1,200.00	
Doubles	£1,500.00		£1,000.00		£1,000.00	
Twin	£1,800.00		£2,000.00		£1,900.00	
Singles	£500.00		£500.00		£500.00	
Bar	£15,000.00		£15,000.00		£15,000.00	
Resturant	£13,490.00		£13,490.00		£13,490.00	
Golf course	£450.00		£450.00		£450.00	
Cleaning		£350.00		£350.00		£350.00
Laundry		£300.00		£300.00		£300.00
Staffing		£15,000.00		£15,000.00		£15,000.00
Food		£2,000.00		£2,000.00		£2,000.00
Drinks		£3,400.00		£3,400.00		£3,400.00
Stationery		£200.00		£200.00		£200.00
Maintenance		£1,500.00		£1,500.00		£1,500.00
Totals	£33,740.00	£22,750.00	£33,640.00	£22,750.00	£33,540.00	£22,750.00
		£10,990.00		£10,890.00		£10,790.00

Pupils / league / Patient 1 / complete graph / simple formulae \ Figures / Graph / Look ups / data / Lottery / Bing

Harry's Hotel

	January		February		March	
	Income	Outgoings	Income	Outgoings	Income	Outgoings
Suites	£1,000.00		£1,200.00		£1,200.00	
Doubles	£1,500.00		£1,000.00		£1,000.00	
Twin	£1,800.00		£2,000.00		£1,900.00	
Singles	£500.00		£500.00		£500.00	
Bar	£15,000.00		£15,000.00		£15,000.00	
Resturant	£13,490.00		£13,490.00		£13,490.00	
Golf course	£450.00		£450.00		£450.00	
Cleaning		£350.00		£350.00		£350.00
Laundry		£300.00		£300.00		£300.00
Staffing		£15,000.00		£15,000.00		£15,000.00
Food		£2,000.00		£2,000.00		£2,000.00
Drinks		£3,400.00		£3,400.00		£3,400.00
Stationery		£200.00		£200.00		£200.00
Maintenance		£1,500.00		£1,500.00		£1,500.00
Totals	£33,740.00	£22,750.00	£33,640.00	£22,750.00	£33,540.00	£22,750.00
		£10,990.00		£10,890.00		£10,790.00

 # MASTERCLASS

Can you change the titles so that they appear sideways to save space?

SKILLS

.: Copy and paste :.

It is very useful to be able to make copies of text, pictures or numbers. It saves time and can prevent errors because there is less typing to do.

You can make copies in a number of ways. The **copy** icon on the toolbar, the **Edit** drop down menu, right clicking or shortcut keys can all be used to produce the same result.

Copy icon   Cut icon

.: Cut :.

To remove unwanted text select the text then click **Edit** on the main menu bar and select **Cut** or click on the **cut** icon.

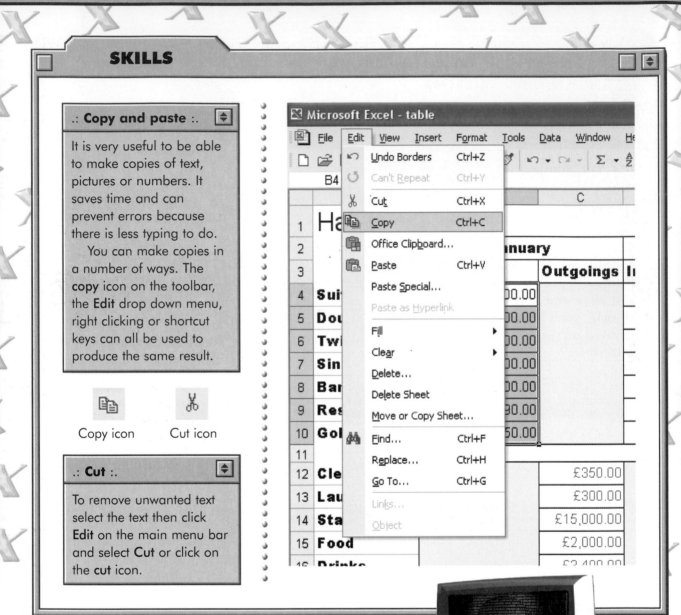

PC MASTER TIP

Always make sure that what you copy is correct so that you do not end up with the same mistake repeated over and over again.

`100100101011010010100101011010010101011101010110111000010101`

 ## SKILL IN ACTION

Harry the Hotelier uses copy and paste to save time setting up his account spreadsheets.

He has to produce cash flow forecasts so he needs to have lots of spreadsheets with the same titles. It would be a waste of time to write the spreadsheet each time so he copies and pastes the basic structure.

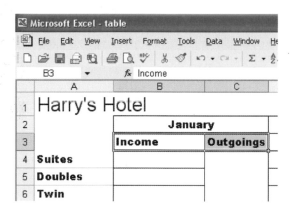

By copying and pasting, he can reproduce the titles again.

EXERCISE

In Excel, draw a star using **AutoShapes** in the **Drawing** menu. Can you copy and paste the star to create a line of identical stars across the page?

Microsoft Excel - table

File Edit View Insert Format Tools Data Window Help

F3   *fx* Income

	A	B	C	D	E	F	G	H
1	Harry's Hotel							
2		January		February		March		
3		Income	Outgoings	Income	Outgoings	Income	Outgoings	
4	Suites							
5	Doubles							
6	Twin							
7	Singles							

11001010110100101001010111010010101010111010101101100001010110

SKILLS

.: Selecting :.

Select the information you want to copy by holding the mouse down as you drag over it. Data will appear with the colour reversed. Images should have a box around them.

Microsoft Excel - table

File Edit View Insert Format Tools Data Window Help

B3 ▾ fx Income

	A	B	C
1	Harry's Hotel		
2		January	
3		Income	Outgoings
4	Suites		
5	Doubles		
6	Twin		

Microsoft Excel - Book3

File Edit View Insert Format Tools Data Window Help

Picture 2 ▾ fx

.: Copying :.

On the menu bar, either click **Edit** then **Copy** or click the copy icon.

.: Pasting :.

Choose where you want the information to go. Put the cursor in the correct place and either click **Edit** then **Paste**, or click on the paste icon.

Paste icon

Microsoft Excel - table

File Edit View Insert Format To

Can't Undo	Ctrl+Z
Redo Paste	Ctrl+Y
Cut	Ctrl+X
Copy	Ctrl+C
Office Clipboard...	
Paste	Ctrl+V
Paste Special...	
Paste as Hyperlink	
Fill	▶
Clear	▶
Delete...	
Delete Sheet	
Move or Copy Sheet...	
Find...	Ctrl+F
Replace...	Ctrl+H
Go To...	Ctrl+G
Links...	
Object	

1
2 Leic
3 Was
4 Harl
5 Sale
6 Sara
7 Bath
8 Nor
9 Glou
10 New
11
12
13 Win
14 Los
15 Dra
16 Bon
17
18

PC MASTER TIP

You can use shortcuts for this: **Ctrl-A** will select all, **Ctrl-C** will copy and **Ctrl-V** will paste. Just hold down **Ctrl** and press the relevant button.

PROGRESS CHECK EXERCISE

Can you copy and paste a cell of data so that it fills 10 more cells?

Microsoft Excel - Book3

	A	B	C
1			
2			
3		John Smith	
4		John Smith	
5		John Smith	
6		John Smith	
7		John Smith	
8		John Smith	
9		John Smith	
10		John Smith	
11		John Smith	
12		John Smith	
13		John Smith	
14			

How could you speed up this process?

Think about copying more than one cell of data at a time. Is this quicker?

Can you copy a group of data?

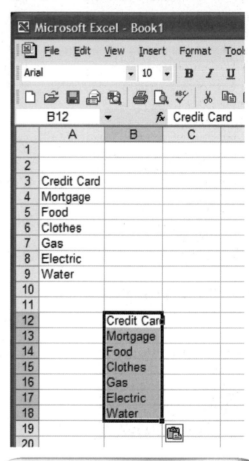

 # MASTERCLASS

Be careful! Once you have stopped copying and pasting, your copied work will be taken off the clipboard. You can lose work this way.

01001010110100010100010101110100010101010101110101010111011100001010110

SKILLS

.: Page setup :.

As explained on pages 12–16, it is extremely important to check what you are printing before you print, especially if you have a large spreadsheet. Many spreadsheets are updates of an original, so it is necessary to label any printout so you can tell the versions apart.

There are a number of different features of the page setup that help you make your work look more professional and can help you keep updates in order.

.: Page setup options :.

There are different ways to set up the page. Margins can be adjusted and the scale can be altered to fit the data on to your page. Header and footer labels can be attached to show the date the spreadsheet was produced, your details, or the name of the file. This is very useful to help keep track of updates.

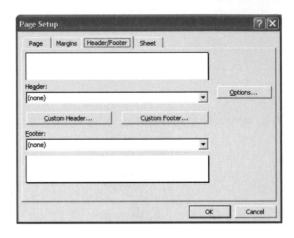

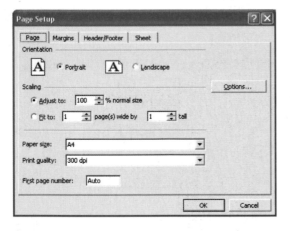

PC MASTER TIP

The header/footer does not appear on your spreadsheet, only on the printout. That is why **print preview** is a useful tool. Remember to check it before printing.

1001001010110100101001011101010101011101010110111000010101

SKILL IN ACTION

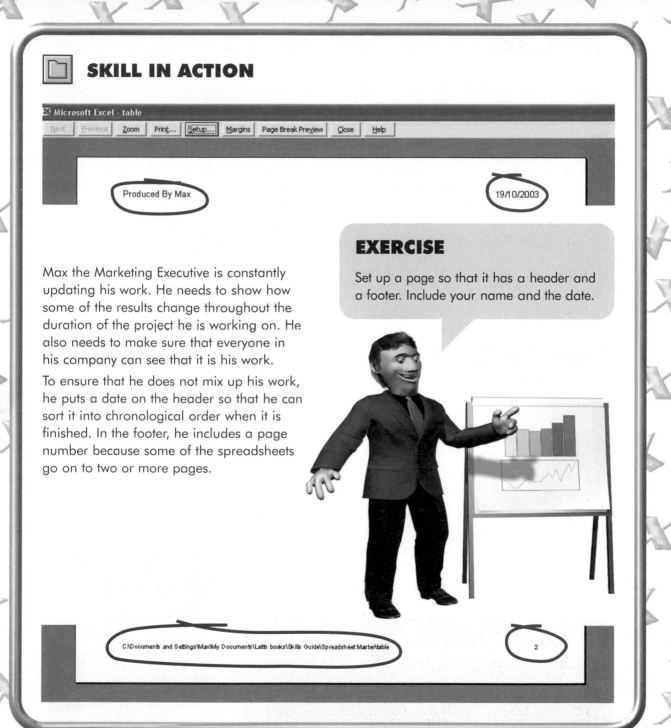

Max the Marketing Executive is constantly updating his work. He needs to show how some of the results change throughout the duration of the project he is working on. He also needs to make sure that everyone in his company can see that it is his work.

To ensure that he does not mix up his work, he puts a date on the header so that he can sort it into chronological order when it is finished. In the footer, he includes a page number because some of the spreadsheets go on to two or more pages.

EXERCISE

Set up a page so that it has a header and a footer. Include your name and the date.

`0100101011010010100101011101001010101011101010110111000010101101`

SKILLS

.: Page setup options :.

All the page setup options can be reached either from the **print preview** icon or from **Page Setup** in the **File** menu.

The Page Setup window has four main features: **Page**, **Margins**, **Header/Footer** and **Sheet**. In the **Page** feature, you can select the orientation of the page and the scaling. To get all of your spreadsheet on one page, select the **Fit to:** option and ensure the page's wide and tall options both have 1 in them.

The **Margins** feature allows you to set exact margins. You can also set where your table or graph will appear on the page.

.: Sheet option :.

We will look at the **Header/Footer** options more closely in the next chapter.

The **Sheet** feature allows you to turn the grid lines on or off, choose the area that you wish to print, and the order in which you wish the pages to print.

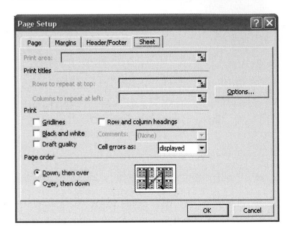

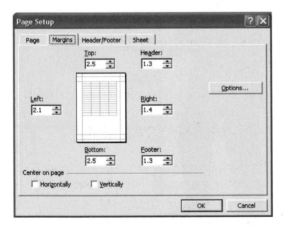

💡 PC MASTER TIP

Always use **Fit to page**. That way you will not waste pages if you make a mistake when printing.

PROGRESS CHECK EXERCISE

Can you fit your work on to one page by using the Fit to: option?

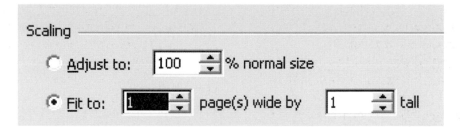

Can you fit a spreadsheet on a page using a percentage reduction?

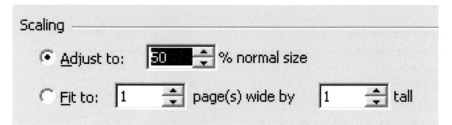

Can you adjust the margins and the centre on Page options so that the spreadsheet appears in the centre of your page?

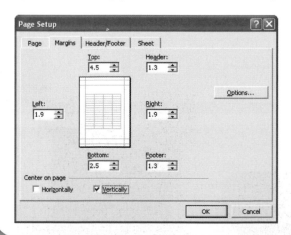

MASTERCLASS

If the page setup shows that you have 1 of 45 pages and you know that you have only one page, can you find the source of the problem?

Hint: Look for a data entry somewhere else on the spreadsheet.

Preview: Page 1 of 45

ADDING A HEADER AND FOOTER

010010101011010010100101011101001010101011101010101011011100001010110

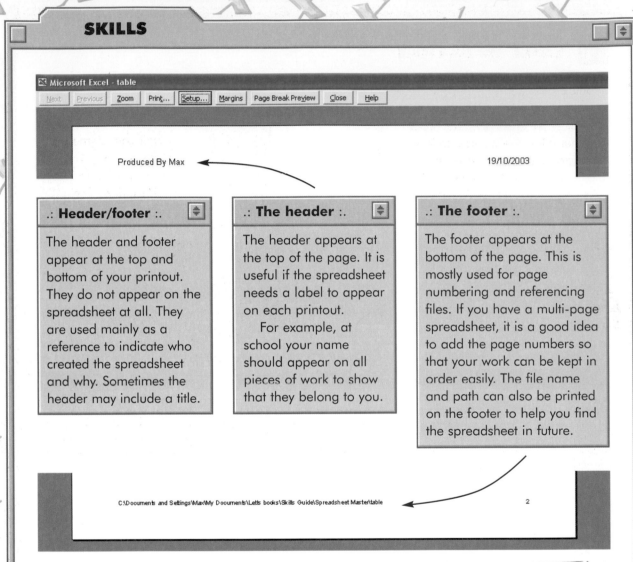

SKILLS

Microsoft Excel - table

Next | Previous | Zoom | Print... | Setup... | Margins | Page Break Preview | Close | Help

Produced By Max ←

19/10/2003

.: Header/footer :.

The header and footer appear at the top and bottom of your printout. They do not appear on the spreadsheet at all. They are used mainly as a reference to indicate who created the spreadsheet and why. Sometimes the header may include a title.

.: The header :.

The header appears at the top of the page. It is useful if the spreadsheet needs a label to appear on each printout.

For example, at school your name should appear on all pieces of work to show that they belong to you.

.: The footer :.

The footer appears at the bottom of the page. This is mostly used for page numbering and referencing files. If you have a multi-page spreadsheet, it is a good idea to add the page numbers so that your work can be kept in order easily. The file name and path can also be printed on the footer to help you find the spreadsheet in future.

C:\Documents and Settings\Max\My Documents\Letts books\Skills Guide\Spreadsheet Master\table ←

2

 PC MASTER TIP

If you add a file name to a footer, you will be able to find the file more quickly when you next want to print it.

SKILL IN ACTION

Sophie the Student has to produce lots of spreadsheets for her course. When she hands her work in to her tutor, she wants it to look professional and she wants her tutor to know it is her work.

Sophie also puts the file path to each spreadsheet on the bottom of each printout because she can never remember where in her filing system she has put each spreadsheet.

She also places the date on each piece of work so that she can keep a record of when she produced it.

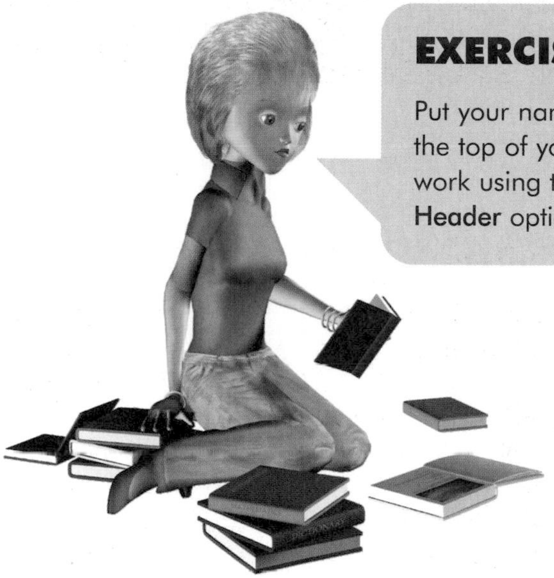

EXERCISE

Put your name at the top of your work using the **Header** option.

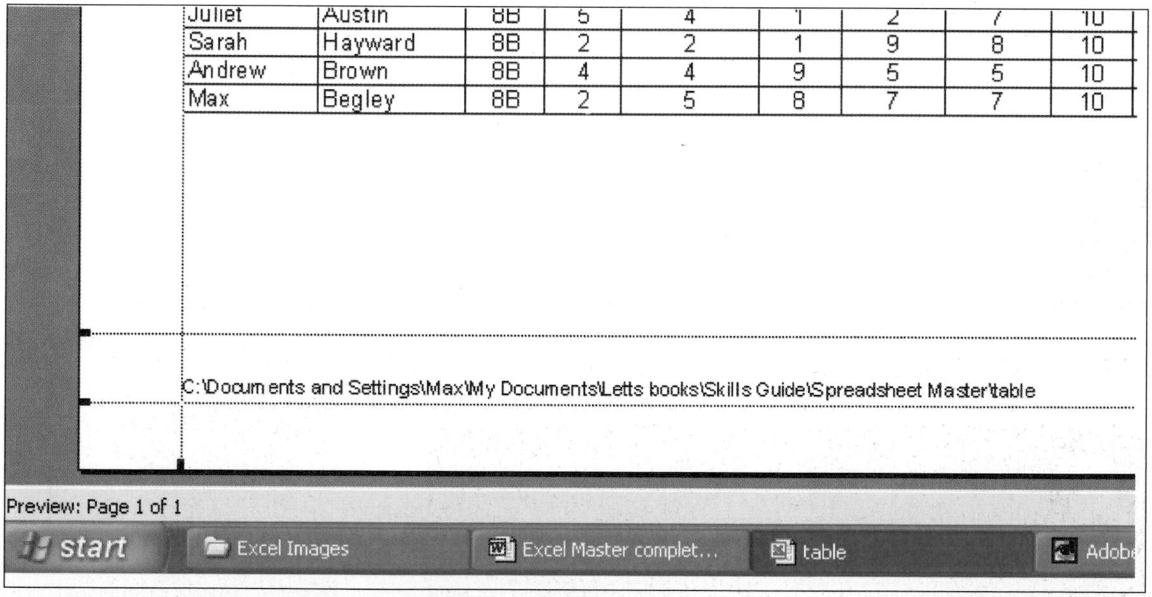

Juliet	Austin	8B	5	4	1	2	7	10
Sarah	Hayward	8B	2	2	1	9	8	10
Andrew	Brown	8B	4	4	9	5	5	10
Max	Begley	8B	2	5	8	7	7	10

C:\Documents and Settings\Max\My Documents\Letts books\Skills Guide\Spreadsheet Master\table
Preview: Page 1 of 1
start
Excel Images
Excel Master complet...
table
Adobe

0100101011010010100101011101001010101110101011011100001010110

SKILLS

.: Headers/footers :.

To insert a header or a footer, select the **Header/Footer** feature in the **Page Setup** window and then choose one of the standard headers from the drop down menu.

Alternatively, you can decide on your own header by choosing the **Custom Header** option.

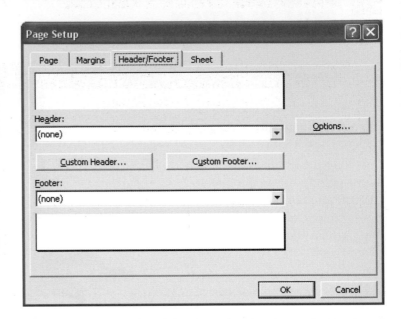

.: Date update :.

There are several icons that automatically update the date and time at frequent intervals and whenever you open the spreadsheet.

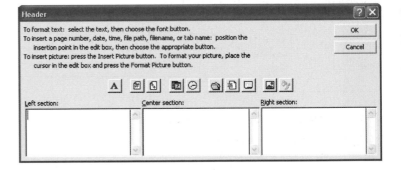

PC MASTER TIP

Try to keep the format of your footers consistent so that the information is clear.

PROGRESS CHECK EXERCISE

Can you insert a header from the options given?

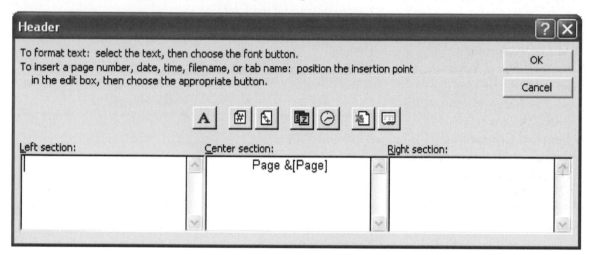

Do you know what all the icons in the Custom Header window do?

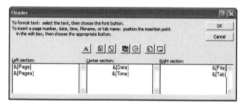

Can you insert a custom header?

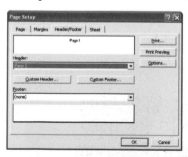

 ## MASTERCLASS

Can you insert a footer that traces the file path so that other people can find where the saved spreadsheet is stored on your computer?

REPLICATION

SKILLS

.: Replication :.

This is very similar to copying and pasting but the computer is trying to guess what you want to copy down the column or across the row.

An example of where this is useful is when you want to put the days of the week in a column. If you type 'Mon' in one cell and 'Tue' in the next and select them both, you can drag down. The other days of the week will be entered for you.

This works with numbers, formulae, dates, days, and months, as well as slightly altered text, e.g. 'race 1', 'race 2', 'race 3' etc.

Microsoft Excel - Book4

File Edit View Insert Format Tools

A2 ▼ fx Week 1

	A	B	C	D
1				
2	Week 1			
3	Week 2			
4	Week 3			
5	Week 4			
6	Week 5			
7	Week 6			
8	Week 7			
9	Week 8			
10	Week 9			
11	Week 10			
12				
13				

PC MASTER TIP

Always double check that the computer is guessing what you want replicated correctly. If you select numbers 1 and 2, it will replicate these two numbers over and over again (12121212). You need to type in 1, 2, 3 to count up.

100100101011010010100101101001010101011101010110110000101010

SKILL IN ACTION

Max the Marketing Executive uses replication to keep track of his spending. He needs to create tables quickly with months across the top row. He saves time by replicating.

He types in the first two months.

	A	B	C	D
1				
2		January	February	
3	Travel	£ 56.00	£ 89.00	
4	Stationery	£ 12.00	£ 10.00	
5	Fuel	£ 84.00	£ 200.00	
6	Accommodation	£ 36.00	£ 178.00	
7	Misc	£ 22.00	£ 55.00	
8	Total	£ 210.00	£ 532.00	

Microsoft Excel - Book4 — C8 — =SUM(C3:C7)

He can then complete the table and copy the formula for calculations down.

Microsoft Excel - Book4 — B8 — =SUM(B3:B7)

	A	B	C	D	E	F	G	H
1								
2		January	February	March	April	May	June	
3	Travel	£ 56.00	£ 89.00					
4	Stationary	£ 12.00	£ 10.00					
5	Fuel	£ 84.00	£ 200.00					
6	Accommodation	£ 36.00	£ 178.00					
7	Misc	£ 22.00	£ 55.00					
8	Total	£ 210.00	£ 532.00	£ -	£ -	£ -	£ -	
9								
10								

EXERCISE

In Excel, produce a column of numbers counting from 1 to 30 using replication. Now try to produce multiples of 5 (0, 5,10,15 etc). Try the same for days of the week and months of the year. Can you create a formula to add the numbers together from the two columns containing numbers? (See pages 40–43) Can you replicate this formula down the spreadsheet?

01100101011010010100101011101001010101011101010110110110000101010110

SKILLS

.: Replication :.

Replication is normally set up to work on a computer when you load Excel, but it is possible to turn it off. To check that it will work, move the mouse to the bottom right-hand corner of a selected cell containing some data. The cursor should change from a thick white cross to a thin black cross. If it does not, you need to change the settings. First, click on **Tools** then **Options** and **Edit**. A menu appears. Click on the box next to **Allow cell drag and drop**. Replicate will work once you have clicked on **OK**.

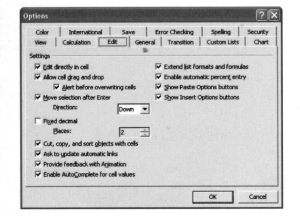

.: Replication :.

You need to type in enough information for the computer to work out what you want to do. This normally means filling two or three cells. If you want a column of even numbers, type '0' in the first cell, '2' in the cell below and '4' in the cell below that. The computer should now be able to guess what you are doing. Select the three cells, move the cursor to the bottom right-hand corner of the last selected cell and drag down the column.

If you are doing this with a formula, you only need to type the formula once. The computer will automatically change the cell addresses for you, e.g. =A1+B1 when dragged down will become =A2+B2 etc.

PC MASTER TIP

Always click on the last cell and check the formula again to make sure it has replicated correctly.

1001001010110100101001011101001010110101010110110000101

 ## PROGRESS CHECK EXERCISE

Can you enable and disable the replication function?

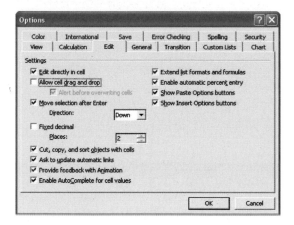

Can you replicate a set of numbers or words down a column?

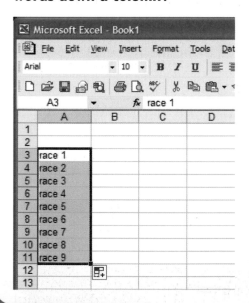

Can you replicate a formula?

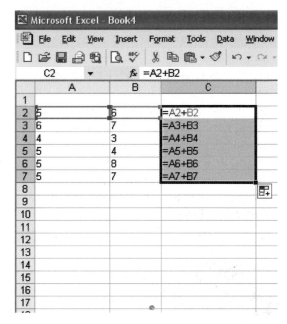

 ## MASTERCLASS

Use the **Help** function in Excel to help you work out how to replicate a formula down a column and across a row.

How can you fix the formula so that only one variable changes, e.g. you want all the numbers to be multiplied by cell C5?

HINT: Look up **absolute cell referencing**. (See pages 56–59)

0100101011010010100101011101001010101011101010110111000010101

SKILLS

.: Drag and drop :.

Placing a piece of data in the wrong cell is common and very frustrating. Drag and drop is a simple way of putting the piece of data in the correct place without having to type it out again. You can do this to a single cell or a group of cells.

It is possible to drag and drop right off the spreadsheet into another application such as Microsoft® Word. However, this takes the cell with it so it is not worth doing if you are dragging a single cell. Dragging and dropping in this way is more useful if you are dragging a list from one application to another because it automatically creates a table the size you need.

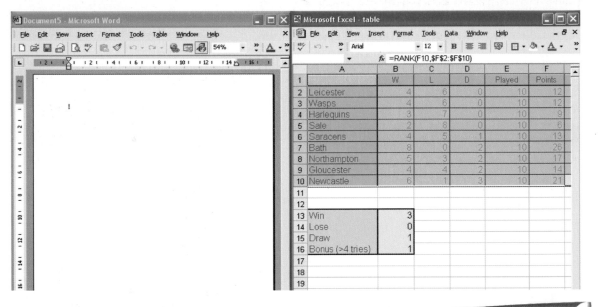

Excel table (Microsoft Excel - table), formula bar: =RANK(F10,$F$2:$F$10)

	A	B	C	D	E	F
		W	L	D	Played	Points
1						
2	Leicester	4	6	0	10	12
3	Wasps	4	6	0	10	12
4	Harlequins	3	7	0	10	9
5	Sale	2	8	0	10	6
6	Saracens	4	5	1	10	13
7	Bath	8	0	2	10	26
8	Northampton	5	3	2	10	17
9	Gloucester	4	4	2	10	14
10	Newcastle	6	1	3	10	21
11						
12						
13	Win	3				
14	Lose	0				
15	Draw	1				
16	Bonus (>4 tries)	1				
17						
18						
19						

PC MASTER TIP

If you press the **Ctrl** key when you are dragging and dropping, the selected data will be copied not moved. A very useful shortcut!

SKILL IN ACTION

Nick the Newspaper Editor uses drag and drop all the time. Sometimes he makes a mistake and puts the data in the wrong place on the spreadsheet. Sometimes he remembers that he needs to add extra information in a table. He drags down some of the table to put in the extra data where he wants it.

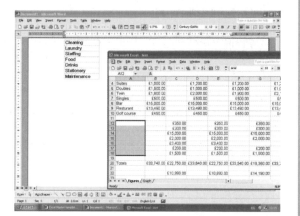

EXERCISE

Can you select a piece of data and drag it to another location on a spreadsheet?

Every now and again Nick produces a large spreadsheet that he wants to put into a report. The report is produced in another application such as a word processor or desktop publishing package. Nick can drag and drop between the two applications but he has to be careful.

010010101101001010010101101001010101011010101101101100001010110

SKILLS

.: How to drag and drop :.

Firstly, select the cell or group of cells that you want to move. Then move your cursor to the edge of the selected area.

Normally the cursor is a small white cross with a black outline. When it is on the edge of the selected area, it turns from a cross to a four-pointed arrow.

.: How to drag and drop :.

Once the four-pointed arrow appears, you can click the mouse. Keep the mouse button depressed and drag the data or group of data to the place where you want it. Then release the mouse button and the data will drop into place.

The diagram shows the two highlighted columns have been moved two columns to the right so that more data can be added.

Microsoft Excel - table

File Edit View Insert Format Tools Data Window Help

D2

	A	B	C	D	E
1	Tom's exam results				
2				%	Grade
3	Art			46	D
4	Business Studies			54	C
5	Design Technology			86	A
6	English Language			76	B
7	English Literature			72	B
8	Geography			36	E
9	German			45	D
10	ICT			80	B
11	Maths			64	C
12	PE			76	B
13	Science			59	C
14	Average			63.091	C
15					

.: Two applications :.

To drag and drop between two applications, minimise the two screens so they are side by side or so that you can see them both. Then just drag and drop!

Remember you will form a table in the second application the correct size and shape. You will find that the solutions to your formulae are shown, but not the formulae themselves.

 PC MASTER TIP

If the cursor is not a black four-pointed arrow, it will not drag and drop. It will either select or replicate.

PROGRESS CHECK EXERCISE

Can you select a group of data?

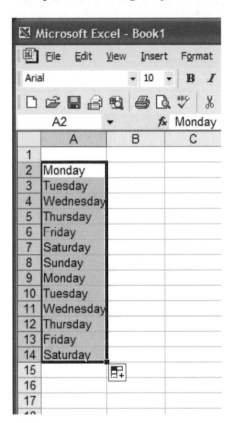

Can you drag and drop a piece of data from a spreadsheet into another application?

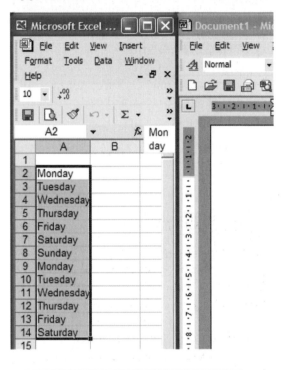

Can you see the change in the cursor from a cross to a four-pointed arrow?

✓ MASTERCLASS

Can you copy and drag?

Hint: Press the **Ctrl** key as you drag and drop.

0100101011010010100101011010010101010110101011011100001010110

SKILLS

.: Simple formulae :.

Formulae are what make the spreadsheet different from a calculator.

Adding a formula to your spreadsheet reduces the time you spend working out any calculation. A formula can be as simple as adding two adjoining cells together or as complicated as one that brings data from many sources to calculate a percentage.

.: Simple formulae :.

A formula is made up of mathematical symbols and cell addresses. For example, adding two cells together might look like this:

=B3+B4

The content of the cells does not matter, as long as it is a number. Therefore if the content of one of the cells changes, the formula automatically calculates the answer to the new sum. It is not necessary to work out a new formula.

Microsoft Excel - Book1

File Edit View Insert Format Tools

Arial   10   **B** *I* U

E23   fx

	A	B	C
1			
2	Exam 1	Exam2	Total
3	10	13	=A3+B3
4	14	20	=A4+B4
5	13	11	=A5+B5
6	14	11	=A6+B6
7	10	14	=A7+B7
8	7	6	=A8+B8
9	4	20	=A9+B9
10	20	16	=A10+B10
11	13	12	=A11+B11
12	11	13	=A12+B12
13	20	17	=A13+B13
14	10	12	=A14+B14
15	13	11	=A15+B15
16	12	11	=A16+B16
17			
18			=AVERAGE(C3:C16)
19			
20			

 PC MASTER TIP

If you are not sure how to type a formula, click on the **function wizard, fx**.

1001001010110100101001011101001010101110101011011100001010

SKILL IN ACTION

Harry the Hotelier has many spreadsheets but he is not very good at maths and he makes a lot of mistakes. To help with this, Harry has made some spreadsheets with formulae in them to do all the maths for him.

Harry can see the formula that he has written in the formula bar at the top of the screen.

Some of the formulae that Harry has written are fairly simple. As he gets more confident using formulae he starts to create much more complicated ones.

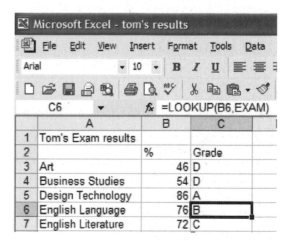

Microsoft Excel - Book1			
File Edit View Insert Format Tools Data Windo			
Arial ▾ 10 ▾ **B** *I* U ▤ ▤ ▤ ▤			
☐ ☞ ◼ ◻ ◳ ◳ ◳ ◈ ✂ ◲ ◱ ▾ ◡ ▾			
C22 ▾ *fx* =B20-C20			

	A	B	C	
1	Harry's			
2			January	
3		Income	Outgoing	Incom
4	Suites	1000		1200
5	Doubles	1500		1000
6	Twin	1800		2000
7	Singles	500		500
8	Bar	15000		15000
9	Restaurant	13490		13490
10	Golf Course	450		450
11				
12	Cleaning		350	
13	Laundry		300	
14	Staffing		15000	
15	Food		2000	
16	Drinks		3400	
17	Stationery		200	
18	Maintenance		1500	
19				
20	Totals	=SUM(B4:B19)	=SUM(C4:C19)	=SUM
21				
22	Profit		=B20-C20	
23				
24				

Microsoft Excel - tom's results			
File Edit View Insert Format Tools Data			
Arial ▾ 10 ▾ **B** *I* U ▤ ▤ ▤			
☐ ☞ ◼ ◻ ◳ ◳ ◳ ◈ ✂ ◲ ◱ ▾ ◡			
C6 ▾ *fx* =LOOKUP(B6,EXAM)			

	A	B	C
1	Tom's Exam results		
2		%	Grade
3	Art	46	D
4	Business Studies	54	D
5	Design Technology	86	A
6	English Language	76	B
7	English Literature	72	C

EXERCISE

Add two cells together using a formula.

01001010110100101001010110100101010101101010101101100001010110

SKILLS

.: Simple formulae :.

The most important thing to remember is that all formulae start with an = symbol. Without the =, the formula will not work.

A simple formula might be adding two cells together. The content of the cell is not important, it is the cell address that matters. To add cell A1 to cell B1 is simply =A1+B1. The formula should be typed in the cell where you want the result to be displayed.

Microsoft Excel - Book1

File   Edit   View   Insert   Format

AVERAGE   ▼ X ✓ *fx* =A1+B1

	A	B	C
1	2	4	=A1+B1

.: Simple formulae :.

The formula will be displayed in the formula bar at the top of the page. In the cell where you have typed the formula, you should get the answer to the problem.

Microsoft Excel - Book1

File   Edit   View   Insert   Format   T

C1   ▼   *fx* =A1+B1

	A	B	C
1	2	4	6
2			

.: Simple formulae :.

If there is an error in the formula, the spreadsheet will tell you in a number of different ways. Sometimes you will see a pop-up window which will either try to point out a solution to the error or display #REF! If this happens, go back and have another look at the formula.

Often it is a simple error. If ###### appears in the cell, then the column needs to be widened as the answer is too long for the cell. Usually this should lengthen automatically. If not, double click on the line between the column labels at the top of the sheet.

💡 PC MASTER TIP

See if you can work out a formula. The computer often suggests that you have done something wrong if there is an error.

101001001010110100101010010101110100101010101110101011011100001010

PROGRESS CHECK EXERCISE

Can you multiply two cells together?

Can you use the word 'sum' in a formula?

	File	Edit	View	Insert	Format	Tools	Data	Window	Help

Arial ▼ 10 ▼ **B** *I* U ≡ ≡ ≡ ⊞ 📇 % ,

☐ 📂 💾 🖨 🔍 🖨 🔍 ✓ ✂ 📋 📋 ▼ 🖌 ↺ ▼ ↻ ▼ 💿 Σ

E2	▼	*fx*	=SUM(A2:D2)

	A	B	C	D	E	F
1	Week 1	Week 2	Week 3	Week 4	Total	
2	2	4	7	12	25	
3						

Can you use the AutoSum function?

If you use **AutoSum**, the computer highlights the cells that will be added. If these are incorrect, you can reselect them.

AutoSum icon   Σ ▼

SUM	▼ X ✓ *fx*	=SUM(A5:B5)		
	A	B	C	D	E
1					
2	Exam 1	Exam2	Total		
3	10	13	23		
4	14	20	34		
5	13	11	=SUM(A5:B5)		
6	14	11	SUM(**number1**, [number2], ...)		
7	10	14			
8	7	6			
9	4	20			

SUM	▼ X ✓ *fx*	=SUM(C3:C4)		
	A	B	C	D	E
1					
2	Exam 1	Exam2	Total		
3	10	13	23		
4	14	20	34		
5	13	11	=SUM(C3:C4)		
6	14	11	SUM(**number1**, [number2], ...)		
7	10	14			
8	7	6			
9	4	20			

MASTERCLASS

Use some of the other options available in the **AutoSum** icon drop down menu.

1100101010110100101001011101001010101011101010110101100001010110

SKILLS

.: Graphs :.

Graphs are one of the most powerful aspects of a spreadsheet. They are very easy to produce and understand.

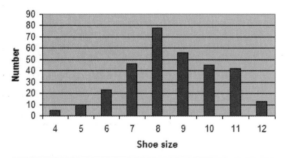

Number of people with each shoe size

.: Creating a graph :.

Creating a graph requires data. This must be in numerical form. If it is not, the spreadsheet cannot convert text into a picture. A simple example of creating a graph is to show the most common shoe size in a class. The data may range from 1 to 30, but it is more likely to have a spread of a few pupils per shoe size.

Microsoft Excel - table

File   Edit   View   Insert   Format

Arial   10   B

K30   fx

	A	B	C
1	Shoe size		
2	4	5	
3	5	10	
4	6	23	
5	7	46	
6	8	78	
7	9	56	
8	10	45	
9	11	42	
10	12	13	

.: Chart wizard :.

Once the data has been selected, it is a matter of working through the **chart wizard**. The icon for this can be found in the top toolbar.

Chart wizard icon

.: Choosing a graph :.

There are many different graphs to choose from. You can edit what the graph looks like after you have constructed it.

PC MASTER TIP

Decide which sort of graph would show the results best. This is the key to a successful graph.

🗀 SKILL IN ACTION

Donald the Doctor has been monitoring several of his patients' heart rates to see if a fitness programme they are on is working. He has entered all the data into a spreadsheet and created two sets of graphs.

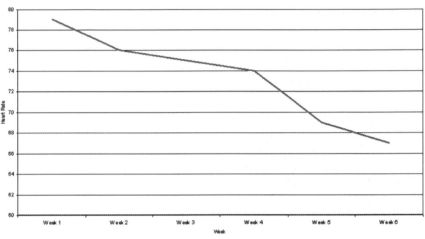

The first set is an individual graph that he can give to each of his patients to show how they have performed.

The second graph shows all the patients' data. This means that Donald can see how each person compared with the others in the programme.

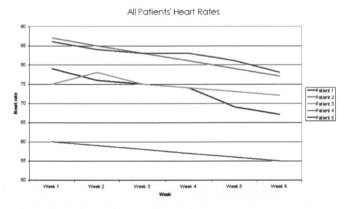

EXERCISE

Produce a simple bar graph comparing three sets of data.

Donald finds the graph useful to show his patients how they are doing.

SKILLS

.: Creating a graph :.

To construct a graph you need some data. The data needs to be in number form otherwise the spreadsheet cannot convert it into a graph. Once you have selected your data, click on the **chart wizard** icon. (Chart is the American word for graph.)

.: Graph wizard (step 1) :.

You will see a new window. This is the wizard and it will take you through making your graph. First, select the type of graph you wish to create. At this point quickly press and hold the sample button to have a look at roughly how your graph will turn out.

.: Graph wizard (step 2) :.

Press **Next**. The selection of cells that you made before starting the chart wizard should be displayed. Now you can label the legend or the key by clicking on **Series** at the top of the window. This will enable you to label each of the series that you have. It is not really necessary if you only have one series.

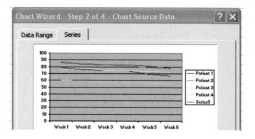

.: Graph wizard (steps 3 and 4) :.

Press **Next** again and you will be able to label the axes, take off the legend and edit the look of your graph.

The last part of the wizard asks you if you want the graph on the same worksheet as the data or a new worksheet. You can label the worksheet here too.

Press **Finish** and your graph will be displayed.

PC MASTER TIP

Try different styles of graph to see which explains the data most clearly.

PROGRESS CHECK EXERCISE

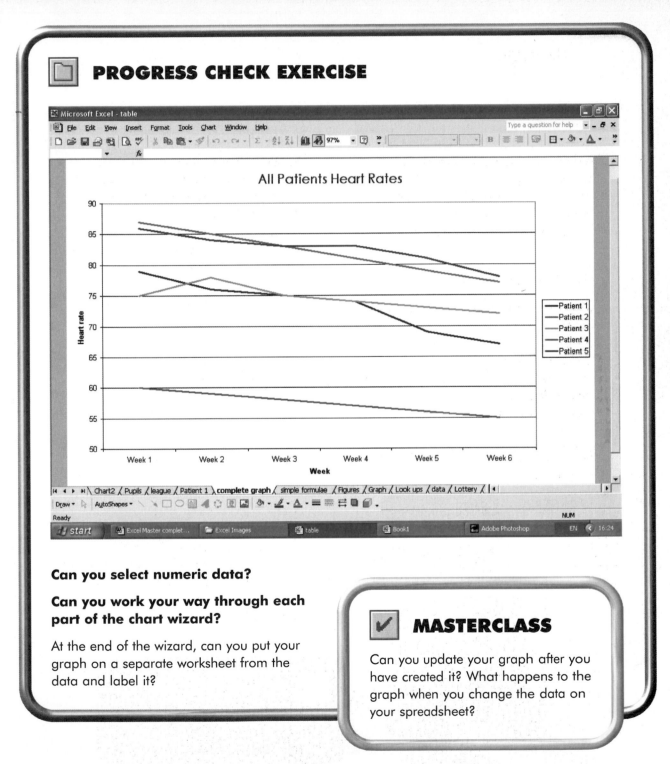

Can you select numeric data?

Can you work your way through each part of the chart wizard?

At the end of the wizard, can you put your graph on a separate worksheet from the data and label it?

✓ MASTERCLASS

Can you update your graph after you have created it? What happens to the graph when you change the data on your spreadsheet?

SKILLS

.: Sorting data :.

Often it is necessary to produce a table of results and draw conclusions from the table. Finding the highest or lowest figure in a table of hundreds of results can be time-consuming and difficult. It is very easy to make mistakes but it is possible to sort a table into an order either alphabetically or numerically.

Microsoft Excel - table

	A	B	C	D	E	F	H
1		W	L	D	Played	Points	
2	Leicester	4	6	0	10	12	
3	Wasps	4	6	0	10	12	
4	Harlequins	3	7	0	10	9	
5	Sale	2	8	0	10	6	
6	Saracens	4	5	1	10	13	
7	Bath	8	0	2	10	26	
8	Northampton	5	3	2	10	17	
9	Gloucester	4	4	2	10	14	
10	Newcastle	6	1	3	10	21	
11							
12							
13	Win	3					
14	Lose	0					
15	Draw	1					
16	Bonus (>4 tries)	1					
17							
18							

.: Sorting data :.

You can sort the table from highest to lowest or lowest to highest, depending on what you require. When the highest is in a cell at the top and the lowest is at the bottom, this is called descending order. If it is the other way round, it is in ascending order.

Microsoft Excel - table

	A	B	C	D	E	F	H
1		W	L	D	Played	Points	
2	Bath	8	0	2	10	26	
3	Newcastle	6	1	3	10	21	
4	Northampton	5	3	2	10	17	
5	Gloucester	4	4	2	10	14	
6	Saracens	4	5	1	10	13	
7	Leicester	4	6	0	10	12	
8	Wasps	4	6	0	10	12	
9	Harlequins	3	7	0	10	9	
10	Sale	2	8	0	10	6	
11							
12							
13	Win	3					
14	Lose	0					
15	Draw	1					
16	Bonus (>4 tries)	1					

.: Sorting alphabetically :.

You can also sort alphabetically, so sorting lists such as a list of football players or members of a class into alphabetical order is easy.

PC MASTER TIP

The variable data in the cells will change when a spreadsheet is updated, so a table will have to be resorted each time it is updated.

1001001010110100101001011101001010101011101010110111000011010

SKILL IN ACTION

Each week Nick the Newspaper Editor needs to put the updated sports leagues in the paper. He has a spreadsheet with all the data in it so each Monday he puts in the latest results and updates each of the tables.

Once he has updated each table, he needs to resort the information so the teams are in the correct order: those with the most points being at the top. This is called sorting in descending order.

Microsoft Excel - table

File Edit View Insert Format Tools Data Window Help

F23

	A	W	L	D	Played	Points	H
1		W	L	D	Played	Points	
2	Bath	8	0	2	10	26	
3	Newcastle	6	1	3	10	21	
4	Northampton	5	3	2	10	17	
5	Gloucester	4	4	2	10	14	
6	Saracens	4	5	1	10	13	
7	Leicester	4	6	0	10	12	
8	Wasps	4	6	0	10	12	
9	Harlequins	3	7	0	10	9	
10	Sale	2	8	0	10	6	
11							
12							
13	Win	3					
14	Lose	0					
15	Draw	1					
16	Bonus (>4 tries)	1					

Microsoft Excel - table

File Edit View Insert Format Tools Data Window Help

F3   fx =B3*$B$13+D3*$B$15

	A	W	L	D	Played	Points
1		W	L	D	Played	Points
2	Bath	9	0	2	11	29
3	Newcastle	6	2	3	11	21
4	Northampton	5	4	2	11	17
5	Saracens	5	5	1	11	16
6	Gloucester	4	4	2	10	14
7	Leicester	4	6	1	11	13
8	Wasps	4	7	0	11	12
9	Harlequins	4	7	0	11	12
10	Sale	2	8	1	11	7
11						
12						
13	Win	3				
14	Lose	0				
15	Draw	1				
16	Bonus (>4 tries)	1				

Nick can then cut and paste each table into his newspaper.

EXERCISE

Randomly type the numbers between 1 and 10 into a column then use the **sort** icon to put them in order.

0100101010110100101001010111010010101010111010101101110000101011

SKILLS

.: Sorting data :.

To sort data, you will need some data to sort. This could be a list of surnames or a list of numbers.

Choose which range of data you wish to sort and then click on one of the cells in that column.

Now click on either the **ascending** or **descending** icon from the toolbar.

A↓Z   Z↓A

Ascending   Descending
icon   icon

.: Sorting data :.

If you have other data connected to the data you wish to sort, it will automatically be sorted with the selected data.

When you have sorted a column of data, check that it has worked correctly and that any related data is still correct.

Microsoft Excel - table

File   Edit   View   Insert   Format   Tools   Data   Wind

B3   fx 46

	A	B	C
1	Tom's exam results		
2		%	Grade
3	Art	46	D
4	Business Studies	54	C
5	Design Technology	86	A
6	English language	76	B
7	English Literature	72	B
8	Geography	36	E
9	German	45	D
10	ICT	80	B
11	Maths	64	C
12	PE	76	B
13	Science	59	C
14			
15			
16			
17			

 PC MASTER TIP

To sort by one column and then by another, use the **Data** link on the toolbar and then select **Sort**.

100100101011010010100101011101001010101011101010110111000010101

 PROGRESS CHECK EXERCISE

Can you sort a list of names into alphabetical order?

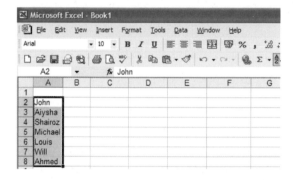

Can you sort a table of results into ascending order?

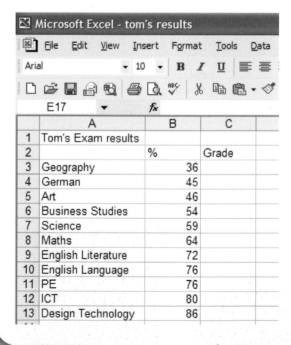

Can you sort a table of results into descending order?

	A	B	C
1	Tom's Exam results		
2		%	Grade
3	Design Technology	86	
4	ICT	80	
5	English Language	76	
6	PE	76	
7	English Literature	72	
8	Maths	64	
9	Science	59	
10	Business Studies	54	
11	Art	46	
12	German	45	
13	Geography	36	

Can you use the sorting tools to find out results such as the highest grade from a list of results?

 MASTERCLASS

Set up a list of subjects, give them a % mark and a grading letter.

Sort the same table of results by each of the columns. Which is easier to read?

SKILLS

.: Goal Seek :.

Sometimes you will need to find a certain result from a formula. **Goal Seek** allows you to set the target result and will change the variables to give the target asked for.

Goal Seek [?] [X]

Set cell: [   ]
To value: [   ]
By changing cell: [   ]

[OK] [Cancel]

.: Goal Seek :.

For example, if you need to know how many matches a team would have to win to reach a certain amount of points, you can find out by using Goal Seek.

.: Goal Seek :.

Goal Seek requires three pieces of information. Two are cell addresses and the other a value.

Goal Seek [?] [X]

Set cell: [$F$9]
To value: [30]
By changing cell: [$B$9]

[OK] [Cancel]

.: Goal Seek :.

Be careful not to get confused over which is a value and which is a cell address.

 PC MASTER TIP

Goal Seek is useful for finding results when there are a lot of variables.

SKILL IN ACTION

Microsoft Excel - table

File Edit View Insert Format Tools Data Window Help

B9   =SUM(B4:B19)

	A	B	C	D	E	F	G	H	I	J
1	Harry's Hotel									
2		January		February		March		April		M:
3		Income	Outgoings	Income	Outgoings	Income	Outgoings	Income	Outgoings	Income
4	Suites	£1,000.00		£1,200.00		£1,200.00		£1,200.00		£5,000.00
5	Doubles	£1,500.00		£1,000.00		£1,000.00		£1,000.00		£4,000.00
6	Twin	£1,800.00		£2,000.00		£1,900.00		£2,100.00		£3,000.00
7	Singles	£500.00		£500.00		£500.00		£500.00		£500.00
8	Bar	£15,000.00		£15,000.00		£15,000.00		£15,000.00		£15,000.00
9	Resturant	£13,490.00		£13,490.00		£13,490.00		£13,490.00		£13,490.00
10	Golf course	£450.00		£450.00		£450.00		£450.00		£450.00
11										
12	Cleaning		£350.00				£350.00		£350.00	
13	Laundry		£300.00				£300.00		£300.00	
14	Staffing		£15,000.00				£15,000.00		£15,000.00	
15	Food		£2,000.00				£2,000.00		£2,000.00	
16	Drinks		£3,400.00				£3,400.00		£3,400.00	
17	Stationery		£200.00				£200.00		£200.00	
18	Maintenance		£1,500.00				£1,500.00		£1,500.00	
19										
20	Totals	£33,740.00	£22,750.00	£33,640.00	£22,750.00	£33,540.00	£22,750.00	£33,740.00	£22,750.00	£41,440.00
21										
22			£10,990.00		£10,890.00		£10,780.00		£10,990.00	

Goal Seek

Set cell: B20

To value: 22750

By changing cell: $B$9

OK   Cancel

Harry the Hotelier uses Goal Seek to see how many rooms he has to fill each month to break even. Breaking even means covering all his costs, e.g. paying his staff, but not making a profit.

He can also use Goal Seek to see how many guests he needs to make a certain amount of profit.

Harry can use Goal Seek to model how much he can make in a certain part of the hotel to keep the rest running at a minimum cost. He finds it very useful in planning future events.

EXERCISE

Copy the table on page 54 and try using Goal Seek for a question of your own.

SKILLS

.: How to set Goal Seek :.

To set Goal Seek, you need to have a table or spreadsheet containing formulae, e.g. the table below:

	A	B	C	D	E	F
		W	L	D	Played	Points
1						
2	Bath	9	0	2	=SUM(B2:D2)	=B2*$B$13+D2*B
3	Newcastle	6	2	3	=SUM(B3:D3)	=B3*$B$13+D3*B
4	Northampton	5	4	2	=SUM(B4:D4)	=B4*$B$13+D4*B
5	Saracens	5	5	1	=SUM(B5:D5)	=B5*$B$13+D5*B
6	Gloucester	4	4	2	=SUM(B6:D6)	=B6*$B$13+D6*B
7	Leicester	4	6	1	=SUM(B7:D7)	=B7*$B$13+D7*B
8	Wasps	4	7	0	=SUM(B8:D8)	=B8*$B$13+D8*B
9	Harlequins	4	7	0	=SUM(B9:D9)	=B9*$B$13+D9*B
10	Sale	2	8	1	=SUM(B10:D10)	=B10*$B$13+D10*$
11						
12						
13	Win	3				
14	Lose	0				
15	Draw	1				
16	Bonus (>4 tries)	1				
17						
18						

.: Using Goal Seek :.

Then you need to ask yourself some questions, e.g. 'What if Wasps won the next four matches? How many points would they have?' or 'How many matches would Newcastle have to win to be top of the league?'

Once you have some questions, you can try out Goal Seek. **Goal Seek** is in the **Tools** menu in the top menu bar. When you have selected it, you will see a new window asking for three different pieces of data.

.: Goal Seek window :.

The first piece of data goes in the **Set cell:** box. This is the cell you want to set to a particular value. Click on the cell you want to change.

The next piece of data you need is the value that you want the set cell to reach. For example, to find out how many matches Newcastle would have to win to be top of the league, the value would be 27 or more because Bath have 26 points.

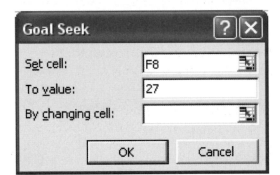

.: Goal Seek results :.

The last piece of data is another cell address. This is the cell you need to change to get your result. In this example, it is the number of matches won (B10). This must be a number. It cannot be a formula.

Click on **OK** and the result will appear. You can try this as many times as you like to get the value you need or the information you require.

PROGRESS CHECK EXERCISE

Can you create some questions that can be answered using Goal Seek?

They should all be 'how many?' or 'how much?' questions because you will be looking for a numeric answer.

For example,

- How many tickets will I need to sell in order to make a profit?

- How much will I need to charge?

- How much butter will I need to make 300 scones?

Can you use the Goal Seek tool to solve the questions you have asked?

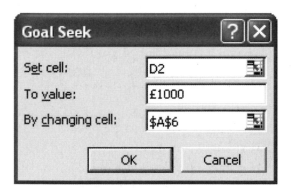

Can you use Goal Seek to work out a simple profit/loss spreadsheet?

 ## MASTERCLASS

Invent a product, some costs and a selling price. Create a simple spreadsheet to show your data. Then try using **Goal Seek** to work out different amounts of profit.

ABSOLUTE CELL REFERENCES

SKILLS

.: Absolute cell referencing :.

Sometimes you may want to copy a formula by replicating it. Normally this is fine as each cell in the formula is related to those in other columns.

However, you may sometimes want to reference a particular cell and keep that cell as the reference all the time, even when replicating.

Microsoft Excel - table

File Edit View Insert Format Tools Data Window Help

F2   fx =B2*$B$13+D2*$B$15

	A	B	C	D	E	F	H
1		W	L	D	Played	Points	
2	Bath	8	0	2	10	26	
3	Newcastle	6	1	3	10		
4	Northampton	5	3	2	10		
5	Saracens	4	5	1	10		
6	Gloucester	4	4	2	10		
7	Leicester	4	6	0	10		
8	Wasps	3	7	0	10		
9	Harlequins	4	6	0	10		
10	Sale	2	8	0	10		
11							
12							
13	Win	3					
14	Lose	0					
15	Draw	1					
16	Bonus (>4 tries)	1					
17							

Microsoft Excel - table

File Edit View Insert Format Tools Data Window Help

F2   fx =B2*B13+D2*B15

	A	B	C	D	E	F
1		W	L	D	Played	Points
2	Bath	8	0	2	=SUM(B2:D2)	=B2*B13+D2*B15
3	Newcastle	6	1	3	=SUM(B3:D3)	
4	Northampton	5	3	2	=SUM(B4:D4)	
5	Saracens	4	5	1	=SUM(B5:D5)	
6	Gloucester	4	4	2	=SUM(B6:D6)	
7	Leicester	4	6	0	=SUM(B7:D7)	
8	Wasps	3	7	0	=SUM(B8:D8)	
9	Harlequins	4	6	0	=SUM(B9:D9)	
10	Sale	2	8	0	=SUM(B10:D10)	
11						
12						
13	Win	3				
14	Lose	0				
15	Draw	1				
16	Bonus (>4 tries)	1				

.: Referencing cell :.

You can do this by **absolute cell referencing**. This tells the computer that you want one cell in the formula to remain constant, even when it is replicated.

PC MASTER TIP

This is excellent for league tables where points are awarded for a win and a draw but not for a loss.

`1001001010110100101010010101110101001010101011101010110111000010100`

SKILL IN ACTION

When Nick the Newspaper Editor set up his spreadsheet for his sports league tables, he used absolute cell referencing to help work out the points. A normal formula would have worked but he would have had to include numbers in the formula.

By using a reference table which is separate from the league table, Nick can just use cell references. However, when he replicates the formula down to the other cells in the column, the formula does not work.

Microsoft Excel - table

F2 = =B2*$B$13+D2*$B$15

	A	B	C	D	E	F
1		W	L	D	Played	Points
2	Bath	8	0	2	=SUM(B2:D2)	=B2*$B$13+D2*$B$15
3	Newcastle	6	1	3	=SUM(B3:D3)	
4	Northampton	5	3	2	=SUM(B4:D4)	
5	Saracens	4	5	1	=SUM(B5:D5)	
6	Gloucester	4	4	2	=SUM(B6:D6)	
7	Leicester	4	6	0	=SUM(B7:D7)	
8	Wasps	3	7	0	=SUM(B8:D8)	
9	Harlequins	4	6	0	=SUM(B9:D9)	
10	Sale	2	8	0	=SUM(B10:D10)	
11						
12						
13	Win	3				
14	Lose	0				
15	Draw	1				
16	Bonus (>4 tries)	1				
17						
18						
19						
20						
21						

Microsoft Excel - table

F10 = =B10*$B$13+D10*$B$15

	A	B	C	D	E	F
1		W	L	D	Played	Points
2	Bath	8	0	2	=SUM(B2:D2)	=B2*$B$13+D2*$B$15
3	Newcastle	6	1	3	=SUM(B3:D3)	=B3*$B$13+D3*$B$15
4	Northampton	5	3	2	=SUM(B4:D4)	=B4*$B$13+D4*$B$15
5	Saracens	4	5	1	=SUM(B5:D5)	=B5*$B$13+D5*$B$15
6	Gloucester	4	4	2	=SUM(B6:D6)	=B6*$B$13+D6*$B$15
7	Leicester	4	6	0	=SUM(B7:D7)	=B7*$B$13+D7*$B$15
8	Wasps	3	7	0	=SUM(B8:D8)	=B8*$B$13+D8*$B$15
9	Harlequins	4	6	0	=SUM(B9:D9)	=B9*$B$13+D9*$B$15
10	Sale	2	8	0	=SUM(B10:D10)	=B10*$B$13+D10*$B$1
11						
12						
13	Win	3				
14	Lose	0				
15	Draw	1				
16	Bonus (>4 tries)	1				
17						
18						
19						

Nick must lock the cells in the reference table so that their reference does not change. Then he can replicate.

EXERCISE

Insert an absolute cell reference into a formula and then replicate it.

EDITOR

SKILLS

.: Absolute cell referencing :.

The reason you need to use absolute cell referencing is to avoid using numbers within a formula. It is usually much easier to create a reference table or cell than to have to change all the formulae because of one number.

The first step is to create your table and work out the normal formula that you would use. The numbers in the formula will be replaced by cell references from the reference table/cell.

12		
13	Win	3
14	Lose	0
15	Draw	1
16	Bonus (>4 tries)	1
17		

.: Absolute cell referencing :.

Now replace the numbers with the relevant cell references, placing a $ symbol on each side of the column letter label from the reference table/cell, e.g. $F$2.

Then you can replicate the formula downward to complete the table.

.: Absolute cell referencing :.

Then create a reference table/cell somewhere else on the spreadsheet that you can use to replace the numbers.

PC MASTER TIP

You can set absolute cell referencing by using the F4 button. If you have selected a cell containing a formula, press **F4** to toggle between the possible absolute references until the one that you want appears.

`10010010101101001010010101110100101010101110101011011100001010`

PROGRESS CHECK EXERCISE

Can you insert the $ symbols in the correct place to lock the reference cells in place?

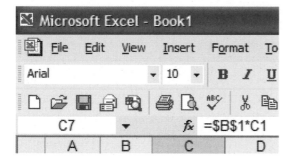

Can you replicate the formula?

```
=$B$1*C1
=$B$1*C2
=$B$1*C3
=$B$1*C4
=$B$1*C5
=$B$1*C6
=$B$1*C7
=$B$1*C8
=$B$1*C9
=$B$1*C10
=$B$1*C11
```

Do each of the formulae work the same way as the first?

Go to **Tools**, **Options**, and check the **Formulas** box is ticked to show your formulae, or hold **Ctrl** and click on to the left of the '1' button.

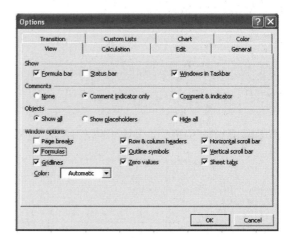

✓ MASTERCLASS

Try including more than one absolute cell reference in one formula. This is when your reference cell needs to become a reference table.

13	Win	3
14	Lose	0
15	Draw	1
16	Bonus (>4 tries)	1

SKILLS

.: Adding columns :.

When creating tables, you sometimes need to add an extra column or row after you have started. This may be for a new group of data or an extra team for example.

.: Adding columns and rows :.

Adding extra columns and rows does not affect any formulae that you might have created.

However, sometimes when you add rows at the bottom of a table, they are not included in any totals that you might have. Make sure you check that they are included.

Microsoft Excel - table

File Edit View Insert Format Tools Data Window Help

	A	B	C	D	E	F	G	I
1		W	L	D		Played	Points	
2	Bath	8	0	2		10	26	
3	Newcastle	6	1	3		10	21	
4	Northampton	5	3	2		10	17	
5	Saracens	4	5	1		10	13	
6	Gloucester	4	4	2		10	14	
7	Leicester	4	6	0		10	12	
8	Wasps	3	7	0		10	9	
9	Harlequins	4	6	0		10	12	
10	Sale	2	8	0		10	6	
11								
12								
13	Win	3						
14	Lose	0						
15	Draw	1						
16	Bonus (>4 tries)	1						

PC MASTER TIP

Select a column by clicking the column label at the top of the column. You can then quickly add extra columns by pressing **Ctrl** and **+** together.

1001001010110100101010010101101001010101011101010110111000010101

SKILL IN ACTION

Tammy the Teacher keeps lists of the hundreds of pupils she teaches on a spreadsheet. She often has to produce class lists and write comments about each pupil. There are some standard tables set up by the ICT department in her school, but sometimes she likes to add her own information about each pupil.

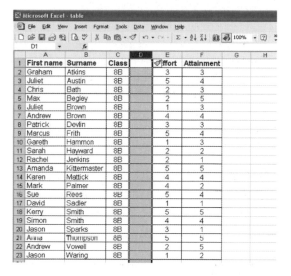

	A	B	C	D	E
	First name	**Surname**	**Class**	**Effort**	**Attainment**
1	Graham	Atkins	8B	3	3
2	Juliet	Austin	8B	5	4
3	Chris	Bath	8B	2	3
4	Max	Begley	8B	2	5
5	Juliet	Brown	8B	1	3
6	Andrew	Brown	8B	4	4
7	Patrick	Devlin	8B	3	3
8	Marcus	Frith	8B	5	4
9	Gareth	Hammon	8B	1	3
10	Sarah	Hayward	8B	2	2
11	Rachel	Jenkins	8B	2	1
12	Amanda	Kittermaster	8B	5	5
13	Karen	Mattick	8B	4	4
14	Mark	Palmer	8B	4	2
15	Sue	Rees	8B	5	4
16	David	Sadler	8B	1	1
17	Kerry	Smith	8B	5	5
18	Simon	Smith	8B	4	4
19	Jason	Sparks	8B	3	1
20	Anna	Thompson	8B	5	5
21	Andrew	Vowell	8B	2	5
22	Jason	Waring	8B	1	2

Tammy wants to add a reading age for the 12/13 year olds in class 8B.

She adds another column in between 'class' and 'effort' and then enters each pupil's reading age.

EXERCISE

Produce a small spreadsheet and then add extra columns and rows.

0100101011010010100101110100101010101110101011011000010101

SKILLS

.: Adding a column :.

To add an extra column or row into a spreadsheet, you need to decide where you want to insert it. Look at the column labels and click on the label to the right of where you need the new column. This selects the whole column.

	A	B	C	D	E	F
1		W	L	D	Played	Points
2	Bath	9	0	2	11	29
3	Newcastle	6	2	3	11	21
4	Northampton	5	4	2	11	17
5	Saracens	5	5	1	11	16
6	Gloucester	4	4	2	10	14
7	Leicester	4	6	1	11	13
8	Wasps	4	7	0	11	12
9	Harlequins	4	7	0	11	12
10	Sale	2	8	1	11	7
11						
12						
13	Win	3				
14	Lose	0				
15	Draw	1				
16	Bonus (>4 tries)	1				
17						
18						
19						
20						
21						

.: Adding a column :.

Using the top menu bar, click on **Insert**, then click **Columns**. A new column will automatically appear. Repeat the process if you need more than one new column.

.: Adding a row :.

It is exactly the same process with rows except that you choose the row below where you want the new row to be.

	A	B	C	D	E	F
1		W	L	D	Played	Points
2	Bath	9	0	2	11	29
3	Newcastle	6	2	3	11	21
4	Northampton	5	4	2	11	17
5	Saracens	5	5	1	11	16
6	Gloucester	4	4	2	10	14
7	Leicester	4	6	1	11	13
8	Wasps	4	7	0	11	12
9	Harlequins	4	7	0	11	12
10						
11	Sale	2	8	1	11	7
12						
13						
14	Win	3				
15	Lose	0				
16	Draw	1				
17	Bonus (>4 tries)	1				

PC MASTER TIP

If you want to add a title above a chart, insert rows above row 1.

PROGRESS CHECK EXERCISE

Can you select a whole row or column?

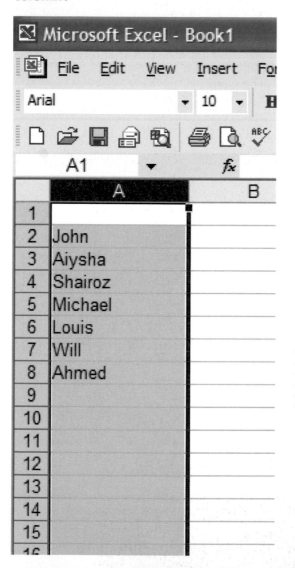

 Can you insert a column in the correct place every time?

If you select the wrong column, you may get the new column in the wrong place. Remember to think which column you would choose if you were adding a column before column A.

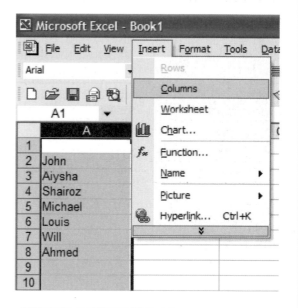

✓ MASTERCLASS

Try the shortcut of selecting a column and then keying **Ctrl** and **+** at the same time to produce the same effect. You can delete columns the same way by pressing **Ctrl** and clicking on the top of those columns.

LOOKUP TABLES

010010101101001010010101110100101010101011101010101101110000101011

SKILLS

.: Lookup tables :.

Lookup tables allow you to relate one set of data with another set of data which is in a separate table. A good example of this is converting an exam result from a percentage to a letter grade A to E.

Exam grades each have a percentage level. For example, to gain a C, a pupil will have to score 50% or over. You can make a table of all the levels.

	A	B	C	D
1	85	A		
2	65	B		
3	50	C		
4	40	D		
5	30	E		
6				
7				
8				
9				

.: Lookup tables :.

On another spreadsheet you may have a list of exam results as percentages. The Lookup table will convert each percentage from a number to a letter automatically. It is important to get the Lookup table the correct way round (descending order) because it will not work otherwise.

Tom's exam results

	A	B	C
1	Tom's exam results		
2		%	Grade
3	Art	46	D
4	Business Studies	54	C
5	Design Technology	86	A
6	English Language	76	B
7	English Literature	72	B
8	Geography	36	E
9	German	45	D
10	ICT	80	B
11	Maths	64	C
12	PE	76	B
13	Science	59	C

PC MASTER TIP

There are hundreds of uses for Lookup tables, from following sports leagues to writing reports.

SKILL IN ACTION

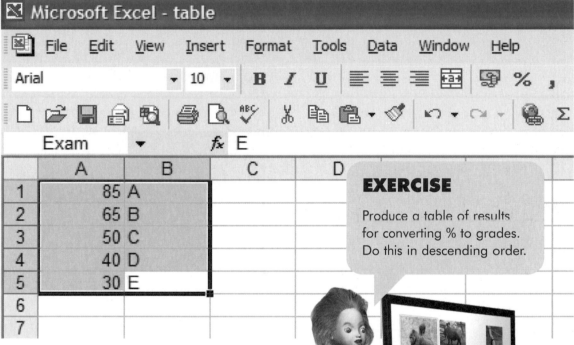

Microsoft Excel - table

File   Edit   View   Insert   Format   Tools   Data   Window   Help

Arial   10   **B** *I* <u>U</u>   % ,

Exam   *fx* E

	A	B	C	D
1	85	A		
2	65	B		
3	50	C		
4	40	D		
5	30	E		
6				
7				

EXERCISE

Produce a table of results for converting % to grades. Do this in descending order.

Tammy the Teacher produces an exam result summary sheet for her tutor group so that they can see their GCSE mock results.

She gets all the results as a percentage from her colleagues and needs to work out the pupils' grades. Firstly, she finds the percentage/grading chart and inputs it into a spreadsheet.

She then produces a Lookup table that does most of the rest of the work for her. Each of her tutor group then gets an individual printout of their mock GCSE grades with the percentage they achieved.

01001010110100101001011101001010101110101011011000010101

SKILLS

.: Producing a Lookup table :.

There are two parts to a Lookup table.

First, there is the Lookup table itself which consists of a value and an answer which will be inserted into the second part of the task. The other part is the spreadsheet which will display the answer.

The Lookup table has two columns. The first is the range of values you want to convert. In this case, it is a percentage exam result. The second column is the answer.

Once you have made the table, it needs to be named. You do this by selecting the whole table and then clicking in the name box in the top left-hand corner of the spreadsheet.

.: Producing a Lookup table :.

On a separate worksheet, produce the spreadsheet that you want to print out.

In the first grade cell (C3), you need to type in the Lookup formula. To start with, use the **Insert** menu. When you are more confident, you will not need to. Click on **Insert** then **Function**. Choose **Lookup** from the **Select a function** list and click **OK**.

.: Producing a Lookup table :.

As this is a simple Lookup table, choose the second option, **Lookup_value, Array**. Fill in the two fields. The first with the cell address of the percentage and the second with the name of the Lookup table. Then finish by clicking **OK**.

Function Arguments

LOOKUP
Lookup_value B3   = 46
Array exam   = {30,"E";40,"D";50,"C

= "D"

Looks up a value either from a one-row or one-column range or from an array. Provided for backward compatibility.

Lookup_value is a value that LOOKUP searches for in Array and can be a number, text, a logical value, or a name or reference to a value.

Formula result =   D

Help on this function   OK   Cancel

.: Producing a Lookup table :.

The finished formula should now appear in the formula bar and the correct answer in the relevant cell. You are now free to replicate the formula down the spreadsheet.

PC MASTER TIP

Lookup tables can be used instead of very complex 'if' statements. The reverse is also true.

100100101011010010100101011101001010101011101010110111000010101

 PROGRESS CHECK EXERCISE

Can you create a Lookup table?

Remember, the table needs to be in descending order.

Can you use the Insert, Function wizard to create the correct formula?

Remember to put the Lookup table on a separate worksheet to avoid confusion. You can put more than one table on your worksheet.

Microsoft Excel - Book1

File   Edit   View   Insert   Format   Tools   Data   Window   Help

E5   =   =LOOKUP(D5,A$3:B$28)

	A	B	C	D	E
1	**CODEBREAKER**				
2					
3	A	1			
4	B	2			
5	C	3		M	13
6	D	4		E	5
7	E	5		E	5
8	F	6		T	20
9	G	7		A	1
10	H	8		T	20
11	I	9		S	19
12	J	10		T	20
13	K	11		A	1

LOOKUP   X √ = =LOOKUP()

LOOKUP
Lookup_value [   ] = any
Array   [   ] = reference

=
Returns a value either from a one-row or one-column range or from an array.

Lookup_value is a value that LOOKUP searches for in Array and can be a number, text, a logical value, or a name or reference to a value.

Formula result =   OK   Cancel

 MASTERCLASS

Can you create a report of three sentences using Lookup tables? If you have a lot of reports to write, Lookup tables save hours of work. Instead of having letters or figures, let the spreadsheet look up sentences.

SKILLS

.: Displaying formulae :.

Sometimes you want to show the formulae that you have used when you print the spreadsheet.

Normally, when you input a formula on the spreadsheet, as soon as you key Enter, only a number appears in the cell. The formula appears in the formula bar at the top of the page.

Microsoft Excel - Book1

File Edit View Insert Format Tools Data Window He

Arial   10   B I U

D20   fx =SUM(D4:D19)

	A	B	C	D
1	Harry's			
2		January		
3		Income	Outgoing	Income
4	Suites	1000		1200
5	Doubles	1500		1000

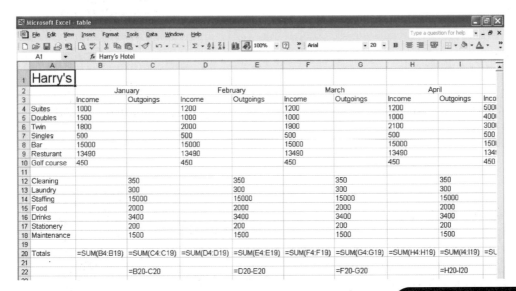

Microsoft Excel - table

File Edit View Insert Format Tools Data Window Help

A1   fx Harry's Hotel

	A	B	C	D	E	F	G	H	I	
1	Harry's									
2		January		February		March		April		
3		Income	Outgoings	Income	Outgoings	Income	Outgoings	Income	Outgoings	Inco
4	Suites	1000		1200		1200		1200		500
5	Doubles	1500		1000		1000		1000		400
6	Twin	1800		2000		1900		2100		300
7	Singles	500		500		500		500		500
8	Bar	15000		15000		15000		15000		150
9	Resturant	13490		13490		13490		13490		134
10	Golf course	450		450		450		450		450
11										
12	Cleaning		350		350		350		350	
13	Laundry		300		300		300		300	
14	Staffing		15000		15000		15000		15000	
15	Food		2000		2000		2000		2000	
16	Drinks		3400		3400		3400		3400	
17	Stationery		200		200		200		200	
18	Maintenance		1500		1500		1500		1500	
19										
20	Totals	=SUM(B4:B19)	=SUM(C4:C19)	=SUM(D4:D19)	=SUM(E4:E19)	=SUM(F4:F19)	=SUM(G4:G19)	=SUM(H4:H19)	=SUM(I4:I19)	=SU
21										
22			=B20-C20		=D20-E20		=F20-G20		=H20-I20	

.: Displaying formulae :.

Using the Tools menu you can set up the spreadsheet to show all your formulae.

Normally you will need to adjust the column widths to fit the whole formula in.

PC MASTER TIP

If you are going to print out your spreadsheet showing the formulae, do not forget to check your **print preview** as it will have changed.

`1001001010110100101001011101001010101110101011011100001010`

SKILL IN ACTION

Microsoft Excel - Book1

File   Edit   View   Insert   Format   Tools   Data   Window   Help

F2   *fx*

	A	B	C	D	E	F
1						
2		Group 1	Group 2	Group 3	Group 4	
3	Week 1	5	6	8	8	=AVERAGE(B3:E3)
4	Week 2	5165	2654	8988	8459	=AVERAGE(B4:E4)
5	Week 3	4	8	12	7	=AVERAGE(B5:E5)
6	Week 4	15	9	15	9	=AVERAGE(B6:E6)
7	Week 5	456	445	654	564	=AVERAGE(B7:E7)
8	Week 6	11	99	45	4	=AVERAGE(B8:E8)
9	Week 7	456	245	854	698	=AVERAGE(B9:E9)
10	Week 8	65	8	88	9	=AVERAGE(B10:E10)
11	Week 9	84	56	57	59	=AVERAGE(B11:E11)
12	Week 10	255	15	32	11	=AVERAGE(B12:E12)
13		=SUM(B3:B12)	=SUM(C3:C12)	=SUM(D3:D12)	=SUM(E3:E12)	=AVERAGE(B13:E13)
14						
15						
16						
17						

In one of her projects at university Sophie the Student needs to show her tutor what formulae she has used to get her results.

The printouts of her normal spreadsheets are fine and look really professional. They have headers and footers referencing the folder on her computer where she keeps the file. However, the tutor must see formulae and does not want to have to look at each student's computer.

Sophie solves the problem by getting the spreadsheet to show the formulae rather than the answers to the problem she has solved.

EXERCISE

Try to show the formulae on a basic spreadsheet.

0100101010110100101001010110100101010101110101011011100001010110

SKILLS

.: Displaying formulae :.

Using the **Tools** drop down menu in the top menu bar, click on **Options**.

.: Showing your formulae :.

Then make sure there is a tick (or check) in the **Formula** box in the bottom left-hand corner of the window. Click **OK**.

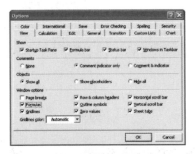

.: Showing your formulae :.

Your spreadsheet should now be showing all the formulae that you have. It will also show the other data but this will remain unchanged. Now you need to adjust the column widths to new sizes because the formulae are usually larger than the answers.

	A	B	C	D
1				
2				
3				
4				
5	3	5	=A5+B5	
6	3	5	=A6-B6	
7	3	5	=A7/B7	
8	3	5	=A8*B8	
9			=SUM(C	
10				

PC MASTER TIP

You can see an individual formula by clicking on the cell. The formula should appear in the toolbar above the spreadsheet.

`1001001010110100101001011101001010101011101010110110000101011`

PROGRESS CHECK EXERCISE

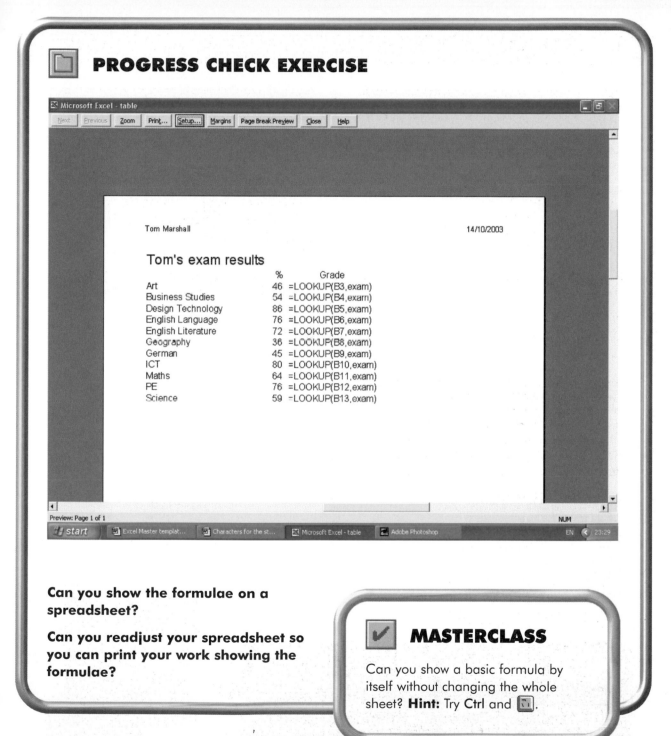

Can you show the formulae on a spreadsheet?

Can you readjust your spreadsheet so you can print your work showing the formulae?

✔ MASTERCLASS

Can you show a basic formula by itself without changing the whole sheet? **Hint:** Try **Ctrl** and ⬚.

AVERAGES

SKILLS

Microsoft Excel - Book1

File   Edit   View   Insert   Format   Tools   Data   Window   Help

A1   *fx*

	A	B	C	D	E	F
1						
2		Group 1	Group 2	Group 3	Group 4	
3	Week 1	5	6	8	8	
4	Week 2	5165	2654	8988	8459	
5	Week 3	4	8	12	7	
6	Week 4	15	9	15	9	
7	Week 5	456	445	654	564	
8	Week 6	11	99	45	4	
9	Week 7	456	245	854	698	
10	Week 8	65	8	88	9	
11	Week 9	84	56	57	59	
12	Week 10	255	15	32	11	
13	Average	651.6	354.5	1075.3	982.8	

.: Averages :.

Often it is useful to work out an average such as the average profit per month. The basic way to work out an average is to add up all the pieces of data you need and then divide them by the number of pieces you have. You can do this by using a simple formula.

Remember, a formula always starts with an = symbol.

PC MASTER TIP

Make sure you do not include any blank cells in the data range as they will affect the final number.

SKILL IN ACTION

For parents' evening Tammy the Teacher wants to tell parents how their child is doing compared with the rest of the class. To do this she needs to work out an average. Then she can see if each child's results are higher or lower than the rest of their class on average.

As she already has the pupils' results in a spreadsheet, Tammy uses an average formula to do the work for her.

Tammy does a quick check to see if her average is correct.

Microsoft Excel - table

File Edit View Insert Format Tools Data Window Help

J2   =AVERAGE(F2:I2)

	A	B	C	D	E	F	G	H	I	J	K
1	First name	Surname	Class	Effort	Attainment	Maths	English	Science	ICT	Average	Rank
2	Jason	Waring	8B	1	2	2	6	10	9	7	5
3	Gareth	Hammon	8B	1	3	8	3	10	3	6	8
4	Patrick	Devlin	8B	3	3	4	9	9	1	6	10
5	Sarah	Hayward	8B	2	2	1	9	8	10	7	4
6	Mark	Palmer	8B	4	2	4	9	8	3	6	8
7	Max	Begley	8B	2	5	8	7	7	10	8	2
8	Anna	Thompson	8B	5	5	5	8	7	5	6	7
9	Juliet	Austin	8B	5	4	1	2	7	10	5	15
10	Amanda	Kittermaster	8B	5	5	4	5	7	3	5	16
11	David	Sadler	8B	1	1	2	4	7	5	5	19
12	Juliet	Brown	8B	1	3	9	4	6	7	7	6
13	Kerry	Smith	8B	5	5	10	10	5	8	8	1
14	Andrew	Brown	8B	4	4	9	5	5	10	7	3
15	Rachel	Jenkins	8B	2	1	2	7	5	9	6	10
16	Karen	Mattick	8B	4	4	7	6	4	5	6	13
17	Graham	Atkins	8B	3	3	2	4	4	9	5	16
18	Andrew	Vowell	8B	2	5	2	1	4	6	3	22
19	Jason	Sparks	8B	3	1	4	7	3	9	6	10
20	Chris	Bath	8B	2	3	8	9	3	2	6	13
21	Sue	Rees	8B	5	4	6	9	3	1	5	16
22	Marcus	Frith	8B	5	4	5	5	3	2	4	21
23	Simon	Smith	8B	4	4	8	2	2	4	4	20

EXERCISE

Input a list of numbers into a spreadsheet, do a quick calculation in your head and work out the rough average. Then work it out using a formula.

0100101011010010100101011101001010101011101010110111000010101

SKILLS

.: Averages :.

Like any other formula, you need some data. In this example we will use Tom's mock GCSE exam results.

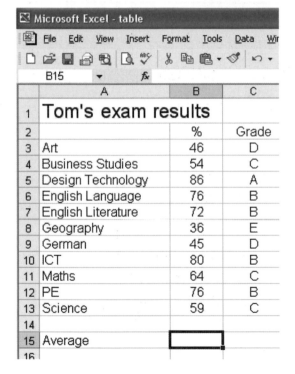

Microsoft Excel - table

File   Edit   View   Insert   Format   Tools   Data   Win

B15

	A	B	C
1	**Tom's exam results**		
2		%	Grade
3	Art	46	D
4	Business Studies	54	C
5	Design Technology	86	A
6	English Language	76	B
7	English Literature	72	B
8	Geography	36	E
9	German	45	D
10	ICT	80	B
11	Maths	64	C
12	PE	76	B
13	Science	59	C
14			
15	Average		
16			

.: Averages :.

There are several ways of inserting an average formula. You can use AutoSum, the drop down menus, or type it in.

Select the cell at the bottom of Tom's results. Then go to **Insert** and **Function** as with the Lookup table. Choose **Average** from the **Select a function** list and click **OK**.

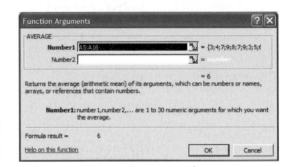

Function Arguments

AVERAGE

Number1   A5:A16   = {3;4;7;9;8;7;9;3;5;6

Number2   = number

= 6

Returns the average (arithmetic mean) of its arguments, which can be numbers or names, arrays, or references that contain numbers.

Number1: number1,number2,... are 1 to 30 numeric arguments for which you want the average.

Formula result =   6

Help on this function   OK   Cancel

.: Averages :.

As this is a simple average formula, select the range you want to find the average of. You will only need to fill in the top line from the two range windows. Then click **OK**. The answer should now appear on your spreadsheet.

PC MASTER TIP

You can also use different types of averages. The word 'average' can be replaced in the formula by 'median' or 'mode' if you want to calculate these.

100100101011010010101011101010101011101010110111000010101

 PROGRESS CHECK EXERCISE

Can you work out the median average?

```
MEDIAN
     Number1  C2                                  = 0
     Number2  C3                                  = 0
     Number3  C4                                  = 0
     Number4                                      = number
                                                  =
Returns the median, or the number in the middle of the set of given numbers.

     Number3: number1,number2,... are 1 to 30 numbers or names, arrays, or
              references that contain numbers for which you want the median.

     Formula result =                    [ OK ]      [ Cancel ]
```

Can you work out the mode?

```
 MODE        ▼  X ✓ =  =MODE(C2:C4)
MODE
     Number1  C2:C4                              = {4;5;5}
     Number2                                     = array
                                                = 5
Returns the most frequently occurring, or repetitive, value in an array or range of data.

     Number1: number1,number2,... are 1 to 30 numbers, or names, arrays, or
              references that contain numbers for which you want the mode.

     Formula result =5                   [ OK ]      [ Cancel ]
```

Can you write an average formula from scratch without using the function wizard?

```
AVERAGE
     Number1                                     = number
     Number2                                     = number
                                                 =
Returns the average (arithmetic mean) of its arguments, which can be numbers or names,
arrays, or references that contain numbers.
     Number1: number1,number2,... are 1 to 30 numeric arguments for which you want
              the average.

     Formula result =                    [ OK ]      [ Cancel ]
```

 MASTERCLASS

Can you use the AutoSum drop down menu to produce an average formula?

SKILLS

.: Ranking :.

If you sorted the list, the rank of the number would be its position in that list.

If using a **ranking** formula, the result given is the rank of a number in a list of numbers. The rank of a number is its size relative to other values in the list.

.: Ranking :.

Ranking gives duplicate numbers the same rank. For example, in a list of data, if the number 8 appears twice and has a rank of 4, then 10 would have a rank of 6 (no number would have a rank of 5).

Microsoft Excel - table

File Edit View Insert Format Tools Data Window Help

A1

	A	B	C	D	E	F	G	H
1		W	L	D	Played	Points	Rank	
2	Bath	9	0	2	11	29	1	
3	Newcastle	6	2	3	11	21	2	
4	Northampton	5	4	2	11	17	3	
5	Saracens	5	5	1	11	16	4	
6	Gloucester	4	4	2	10	14	5	
7	Leicester	4	6	1	11	13	6	
8	Wasps	4	7	0	11	12	7	
9	Harlequins	4	7	0	11	12	7	
10	Sale	2	8	1	11	7	9	
11								
12								
13	Win	3						
14	Lose	0						
15	Draw	1						
16	Bonus (>4 tries)	1						

 PC MASTER TIP

Remember to use absolute cell referencing when replicating a ranking formula. (See page 56)

100100101011010010101001010111010010101010111010101101110000101 0

 ## SKILL IN ACTION

When Tammy the Teacher is writing reports she must give each pupil's position in the class. Tammy thought at first this was going to take her ages, but then she remembered that she had all the data on a spreadsheet.

Tammy remembered ranking things in order from university, so using the Help menu she set about ranking each class list. First she made a formula to work out the average score between Maths, English, Science and ICT. Then using those figures she created a rank formula to rank the classes in order from one to twenty-two.

Tammy then realised that she could sort the table and show it in rank order.

EXERCISE

Make a list of ten numbers and rank them.

0100101011010010100101011010010101011101010101101110000101011

SKILLS

.: How to rank :.

Ranking is a formula similar to average or a Lookup table. First, create a column in the table that you wish to rank, then key in =RANK(to the cell corresponding to the top of the table. This tells the spreadsheet that from now on you are creating a rank formula. The spreadsheet is expecting two pieces of data. The first is the cell you wish to rank and the second is the range of cells that you wish to rank the cell against.

.: How to rank :.

You need to place a comma in between the two pieces of data to keep them apart. So the finished formula should be like this =RANK(J2,J2:J23). The ranking should now appear in the cell. Note that there are no spaces in the formula.

Before the formula can be replicated, you must put in an absolute cell reference to stop the spreadsheet ranking incorrect data. The new formula should look like this: =RANK(J2,$J$2:$J$23). This will lock the data range in place. Then you can replicate your formula. It is then possible to sort your table in rank order.

F	G	H	I	J	K
aths	English	Science	ICT	Average	Rank
2	6	10	9	7	NK(J2,
8	3	10	3	6	
4	9	9	1	6	
1	9	8	10	7	
4	9	8	3	6	
8	7	7	10	8	
5	8	7	5	6	
1	2	7	10	5	
4	5	7	3	5	
2	4	7	5	5	

G	H	I	J	K
glish	Science	ICT	Average	Rank
	10	9	=AVERAGE(F2:I2)	=RANK(J2,J2:J23)
	10	3	=AVERAGE(F3:I3)	=RANK(J3,J3:J24)
	9	1	=AVERAGE(F4:I4)	=RANK(J4,J4:J25)
	8	10	=AVERAGE(F5:I5)	=RANK(J5,J5:J26)
	8	3	=AVERAGE(F6:I6)	=RANK(J6,J6:J27)
	7	10	=AVERAGE(F7:I7)	=RANK(J7,J7:J28)
	7	5	=AVERAGE(F8:I8)	=RANK(J8,J8:J29)
	7	10	=AVERAGE(F9:I9)	=RANK(J9,J9:J30)
	7	3	=AVERAGE(F10:I10)	=RANK(J10,J10:J31)
	7	5	=AVERAGE(F11:I11)	=RANK(J11,J11:J32)
	6	7	=AVERAGE(F12:I12)	=RANK(J12,J12:J33)
	5	8	=AVERAGE(F13:I13)	=RANK(J13,J13:J34)
	5	10	=AVERAGE(F14:I14)	=RANK(J14,J14:J35)
	5	9	=AVERAGE(F15:I15)	=RANK(J15,J15:J36)

PC MASTER TIP

You can also rank by sorting the spreadsheet into order and then numbering the column using replication. (See page 36)

1001001010110100101001011101001010101110101011011100001010

PROGRESS CHECK EXERCISE

Microsoft Excel - table

File   Edit   View   Insert   Format   Tools   Data   Window   Help

G2   *fx* =RANK(F2,$F$2:$F$10)

	A	B	C	D	E	F	G
1		W	L	D	Played	Points	Rank
2	Bath	9	0	2	11	29	1
3	Newcastle	6	2	3	11	21	2
4	Northampton	5	4	2	11	17	3
5	Saracens	5	5	1	11	16	4
6	Gloucester	4	4	2	10	14	5
7	Leicester	4	6	1	11	13	6
8	Wasps	4	7	0	11	12	7
9	Harlequins	4	7	0	11	12	7
10	Sale	2	8	1	11	7	9
11							
12							
13	Win	3					
14	Lose	0					
15	Draw	1					
16	Bonus (>4 tries)	1					

Can you create a simple rank formula?

Can you include an absolute cell reference into the original formula?

Can you replicate the formula to rank all the data in the range and then sort it into rank order?

 MASTERCLASS

Can you get the ranking the other way around for the lowest score?
Hint: place an extra piece of data at the end of the formula so it includes 10.

0100101011010010101010111010010101011101010110110000101011

SKILLS

.: Protecting worksheets :.

There are times when you want to keep the data and the structure of a spreadsheet protected. Using the **protection** tool is similar to having a 'read only' template. A user of the worksheet can add data within limitations set up by the person who made the spreadsheet.

.: Passwords :.

There are four ways to protect your worksheets. The first is to put a password on the sheet so that no one can use it except the people who know the password. The other options allow users a certain amount of access to features dictated by the creator.

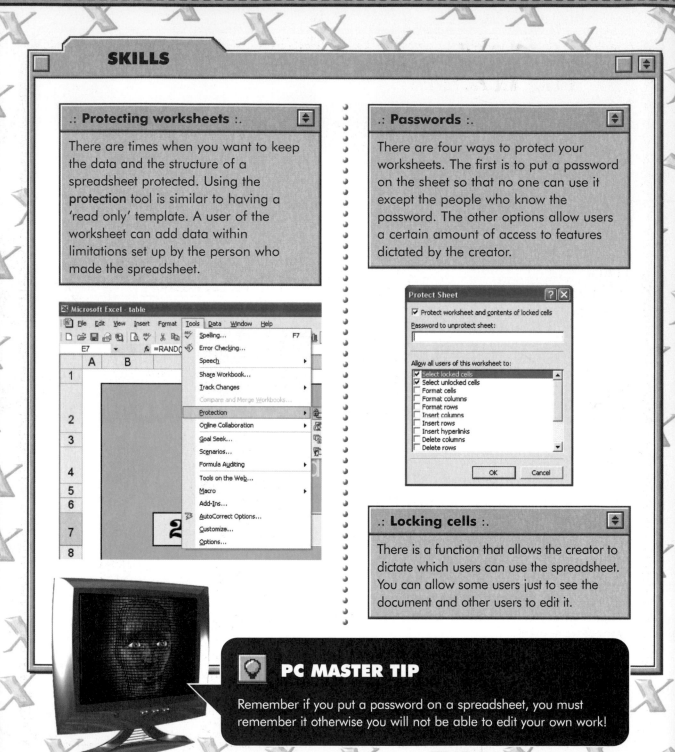

.: Locking cells :.

There is a function that allows the creator to dictate which users can use the spreadsheet. You can allow some users just to see the document and other users to edit it.

PC MASTER TIP

Remember if you put a password on a spreadsheet, you must remember it otherwise you will not be able to edit your own work!

10010010101011010010100101101010101010101011010101101110000101 0

SKILL IN ACTION

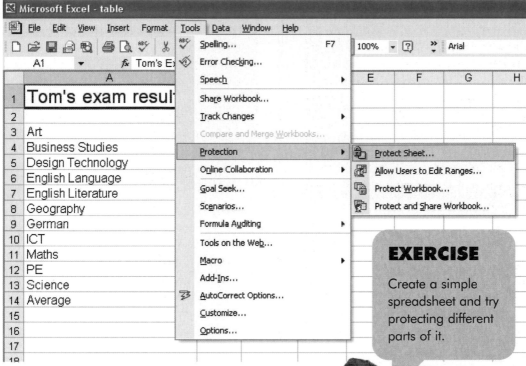

| Microsoft Excel - table |

File Edit View Insert Format Tools Data Window Help

Spelling...   F7
Error Checking...
Speech   ▶
Share Workbook...
Track Changes   ▶
Compare and Merge Workbooks...
Protection   ▶   🔒 Protect Sheet...
Online Collaboration   ▶   Allow Users to Edit Ranges...
Goal Seek...   Protect Workbook...
Scenarios...   Protect and Share Workbook...
Formula Auditing   ▶
Tools on the Web...
Macro   ▶
Add-Ins...
AutoCorrect Options...
Customize...
Options...

A1   Tom's E

	A	E	F	G	H
1	Tom's exam resul				
2					
3	Art				
4	Business Studies				
5	Design Technology				
6	English Language				
7	English Literature				
8	Geography				
9	German				
10	ICT				
11	Maths				
12	PE				
13	Science				
14	Average				
15					
16					
17					
18					

EXERCISE

Create a simple spreadsheet and try protecting different parts of it.

In one of her lessons Tammy the Teacher wants her pupils to use a spreadsheet that she has prepared. There are a lot of complicated formulae on the sheet and Tammy does not want it altered.

Tammy uses the protection feature to stop her pupils changing the data or losing the formulae accidentally.

She has a number of choices but chooses to protect the whole spreadsheet. This makes it impossible to change anything on the spreadsheet without a password.

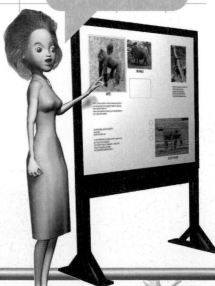

SKILLS

.: Permissions :.

It is possible to set up the protection so that only certain user can have access to the protected areas of the worksheet. This means that you do not have to give out the password to these users, they will be able to edit the sheet. Any problems can also be referred to them as well as you.

Allow Users to Edit Ranges

Ranges unlocked by a password when sheet is protected:

Title	Refers to cells
Range1	$B$3:$B$14

New...
Modify...
Delete

Specify who may edit the range without a password:

Permissions...

☐ Paste permissions information into a new workbook

Protect Sheet...   OK   Cancel   Apply

Protect Sheet

☑ Protect worksheet and contents of locked cells

Password to unprotect sheet:

Allow all users of this worksheet to:

☑ Select locked cells
☑ Select unlocked cells
☐ Format cells
☐ Format columns
☐ Format rows
☐ Insert columns
☐ Insert rows
☐ Insert hyperlinks
☐ Delete columns
☐ Delete rows

OK   Cancel

.: Locking cells :.

You will be prompted to confirm your password and be told to keep a note of it somewhere safe. Your whole spreadsheet is now protected.

Using the protection feature window it is possible to lock certain ranges or groups of cell to allow a certain amount of access.

Remember to note down any password in a safe place.

.: Protection feature :.

To protect the whole spreadsheet, go to the top menu bar and choose the **Protection** feature from the **Tools** drop down menu. Then place a password in the field of the new window.

 PC MASTER TIP

You need to know your password to unprotect the worksheet.

PROGRESS CHECK EXERCISE

Can you set up a workbook so that only certain people can alter the protected area?

Can you copy the permissions from one workbook to another?'

☑ Paste permissions information into a new workbook

Protect Sheet...   OK   Cancel   Apply

Can you set up a spreadsheet so that only the cells containing formulae are protected?

Microsoft Excel ⊠

⚠ The cell or chart you are trying to change is protected and therefore read-only.

To modify a protected cell or chart, first remove protection using the Unprotect Sheet command (Tools menu, Protection submenu). You may be prompted for a password.

OK

Can you protect a complete spreadsheet with a password?

Can you use the protection feature window to allow access to certain parts of a spreadsheet?

 MASTERCLASS

Could you use the protection field to add security to all your files?

SKILLS

.: Editing a graph :.

Once you have produced a graph using the chart wizard, you will probably want to edit it.

.: Editing graph colours :.

There may be several things you want to change. The main features of the graph are the font and the colours. Try and get a good balance of colour, using a different colour to highlight any point you are trying to make, the highest column for instance.

.: Editing graph fonts :.

Try to make the font as readable as possible without being too large or too small.

Before editing

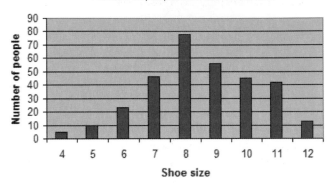

Number of people with each shoe size

After editing

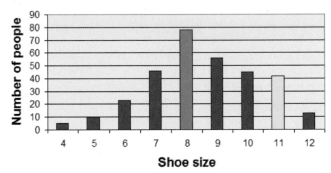

Number of people with each shoe size

PC MASTER TIP

Remember a graph must have a title, labelled axes and a scale. Without these, the graph does not mean anything.

1001001010110100101001011101001010101110101011011100001010

 ## SKILL IN ACTION

Donald the Doctor has created graphs to monitor his patients' heart rate over a series of weeks. He wants to make them easier to read. Some of the colours do not stand out enough to be read clearly and the background of the graphs is rather dull.

Donald decides to edit the graphs. First he gives the graphs a white background so that each heart rate line is easily seen against it.

On the main graph that shows all the patients in the fitness test, he changes the colours of the heart rate lines so they stand out clearly against the white background and can be distinguished from one another.

Donald also wants to make the title stand out so it is easier to see what the graph is about. He changes the size of the font to make it larger than any other text on the page.

Before editing

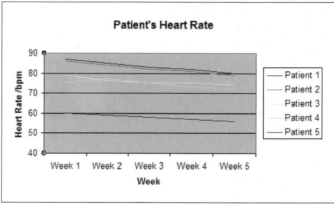

EXERCISE

Change the colours on a graph so that they stand out well.

After editing

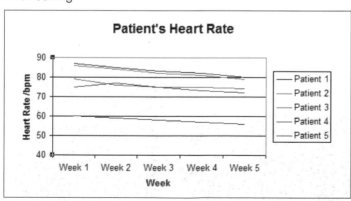

SKILLS

.: Edit the graph background :.

Once you have created the graph, you can change its look. There are several parts of the graph that you can change: they are mainly the colour and style of the text.

To change the background colour, double click on the graph where there is no line or axis. A window will appear that allows you to choose the style and colour of the surrounding border, and the background colour of the graph.

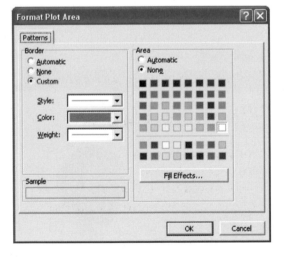

.: Edit the graph text :.

The next part that you can edit is the text.

All the pieces of text on the graph are in small text boxes. By double clicking on each, you can change the size, colour and font of the text. You can also change the alignment of the text. This is particularly useful if your labels do not fit the axis well.

.: Edit the scale and line weight :.

In the same window, you can also change the scale on the axes to show a particular part of the results in more detail or to make the graph clearer.

Finally, it is possible to change the weight, colour and style of the line by double clicking on the results line. You also have the option of adding extra lines to explain the graph better.

 PC MASTER TIP

Everything on the graph can be changed so do not be afraid to experiment.

PROGRESS CHECK EXERCISE

Can you produce a clear graph?

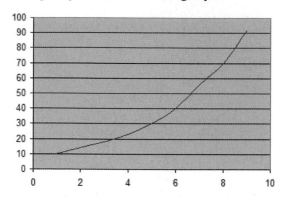

Can you change the type of graph that you are showing?

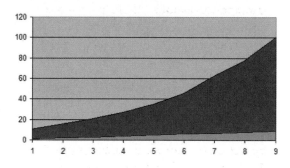

Can you change the font, size and alignment of the axes labels?

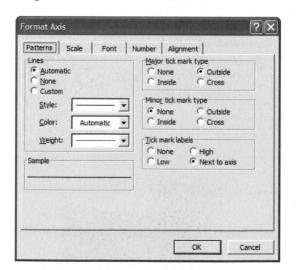

MASTERCLASS

Can you change a graph so that a number of data lines are clear to read and you can distinguish between the lines by using a legend?

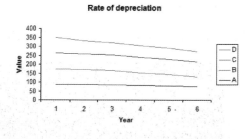

FORMATTING CELLS (CONDITIONAL)

SKILLS

.: Conditional formatting :.

To make text stand out, you can format all the text in a cell or selected characters.

Microsoft Excel

File Edit View Insert Format Tools Data Window Help

E11

table

	A	B	C
1	Tom's exam results		
2		%	Grade
3	Art	46	D
4	Business Studies	54	C
5	Design Technology	86	A
6	English Language	76	B
7	English Literature	72	B
8	Geography	36	E
9	German	45	D
10	ICT	80	B
11	Maths	64	C
12	PE	76	B
13	Science	59	C
14	Average	63.091	C
15			
16			
17			

.: Conditional formatting :.

Conditional formatting is a format such as cell shading or font colour that the spreadsheet will automatically apply to cells if a specified condition is true.

.: Conditional formatting :.

To help show the different types of information in a worksheet, you can put borders around cells, shade cells with a background colour, or shade cells with a colour pattern if the contents of that cell reach a certain value.

Conditional Formatting

Condition 1

Cell Value Is between 85 and 100

Preview of format to use when condition is true: AaBbCcYyZz Format...

Condition 2

Cell Value Is less than 50

Preview of format to use when condition is true: AaBbCcYyZz Format...

Add >> Delete... OK Cancel

PC MASTER TIP

Using conditional formatting the text can appear differently on the page if certain values are reached.

100100101011010010100101110100101010111010101101100001010

SKILL IN ACTION

Tammy the Teacher likes to make the high scores of her pupils stand out on her spreadsheet. She uses conditional formatting to do this so she does not have to search through hundreds of numbers to find the top scores.

Tammy sets the criteria that a percentage of 81 or above is written in blue and the cell is coloured light blue, a percentage of less than 50 is highlighted in red. She can then easily see the higher and lower scores and talk to the child about their performance in each subject. As well as changing the shading of the cell and the font colour, she could also have changed the font itself, the size of the font or the cell border colour.

	A	B
1	Tom's Exam results	
2		%
3	Art	46
4	Business Studies	54
5	Design Technology	86
6	English Language	76
7	English Literature	72
8	Geography	36
9	German	45
10	ICT	80
11	Maths	64
12	PE	76
13	Science	59

EXERCISE

Set some criteria for several cells on a spreadsheet then put in various values to see if they work.

SKILLS

.: Formatting cells :.

First, select the range of cells that you want and choose **Format** from the top menu bar, then **Conditional Formatting** from the drop down menu.

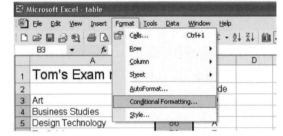

.: Formatting cells :.

Now put in the criteria that your highlighted cell must reach in the fields in the **Conditional Formatting** window, in this case 85 to 100 to highlight a grade A.

.: Formatting cells :.

Then set the format that you wish the data that meets the criteria to look like.

.: Formatting cells :.

Now click **OK**. The cells in the range that meet your criteria will be shown with the new format.

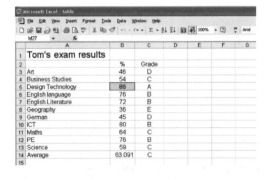

PC MASTER TIP

This sometimes happens automatically. See what happens if a currency cell holds a negative value.

1001001010110100101001011101001010101110101011011100001010

 PROGRESS CHECK EXERCISE

	Microsoft Excel - table				
	File Edit View Insert Format Tools Data Window Help				

L24   *fx*

	A	B	C	D	E
1	Tom's exam results				
2		%	Grade		
3	Art	**46**	D		
4	Business Studies	54	C		
5	Design Technology	**86**	A		
6	English Language	76	B		
7	English Literature	72	B		
8	Geography	**36**	E		
9	German	**45**	D		
10	ICT	80	B		
11	Maths	64	C		
12	PE	76	B		
13	Science	59	C		
14	Average	63.091	C		

Can you set a conditional format to a cell?

Can you add more than one conditional format to a cell?

 MASTERCLASS

Use conditionally formatted ranges of cells to enhance any spreadsheets you produce. This could help you spot an error in your work if you limit the criteria of some cells.

EXPORTING TABLES

`01001010101101001010100101011010010101010111010101011010111000010101011`

SKILLS

.: Exporting tables :.

Although it is possible to create tables in other applications, it is much easier to create a table using a spreadsheet. You can then move it from the spreadsheet and place it into the other application. This is called **integration**.

.: Exporting tables :.

Once the table has been transferred, you can edit the table in spreadsheet form from the second application.

	W	L	D	Played	Points	Rank
Leicester	4	6	0	10	12	6
Wasps	4	6	0	10	12	6
Harlequins	3	7	0	10	9	8
Sale	2	8	0	10	6	9
Saracens	4	5	1	10	13	5
Bath	8	0	2	10	26	1
Northampton	5	3	2	10	17	3
Gloucester	4	4	2	10	14	4
Newcastle	6	1	3	10	21	2

	W	L	D	Played	Points	Rank
Leicester	4	6	0	10	12	6
Wasps	4	6	0	10	12	6
Harlequins	3	7	0	10	9	8
Sale	2	8	0	10	6	9
Saracens	4	5	1	10	13	5
Bath	8	0	2	10	26	1
London Irish	5	3	2	10	17	3
Gloucester	4	4	2	10	14	4
Newcastle	6	1	3	10	21	2

PC MASTER TIP

Do not forget that if you have used any Lookup tables or references elsewhere on your original spreadsheet, these will have to be transferred too.

1001001010110100101001011101001010101011101010110111000011010

SKILL IN ACTION

	A	B	C	D	E	F	G
1		W	L	D	Played	Points	Rank
2	Leicester	4	6	0	10	0	1
3	Wasps	4	6	0	10	0	1
4	Harlequins	3	7	0	10	0	1
5	Sale	2	8	0	10	0	1
6	Saracens	4	5	1	10	0	1
7	Bath	8	0	2	10	0	1
8	Northampton	5	3	2	10	=B8*$B$13+D8*	
9	Gloucester	4	4	2	10	$B$15	
10	Newcastle	6	1	3	10	0	1

Sheet1

Nick the Newspaper Editor creates a lot of spreadsheets. He also produces a lot of reports which contain parts of his spreadsheets. Sometimes he puts the spreadsheets he produces into the newspaper.

If you simply copy and paste a range of cells into another application, then you will lose the use of any formulae. This can be a problem if you want to update it later.

Nick has found it possible to export a spreadsheet to another application so that when he updates the spreadsheet it automatically updates the table in the other application.

EXERCISE

Create a spreadsheet in another application and copy and paste a spreadsheet table into it.

EDITOR

SKILLS

.: Exporting tables :.

Exporting a spreadsheet into another application can be done in two ways. If you select some data and then copy and paste it across, you will lose the formula and therefore find it difficult to edit.

In some applications you can create a spreadsheet from an icon in the toolbar.

Insert Microsoft Excel Worksheet icon

.: Spreadsheet choices :.

By clicking the icon, a drop down menu will give you options on the size of your spreadsheet.

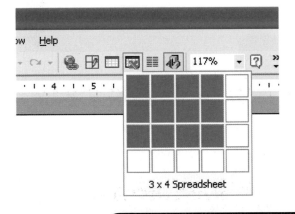

3 x 4 Spreadsheet

.: Sizing the spreadsheet :.

Decide how big you want your spreadsheet and it will appear on your page. Do not worry if you need a larger one: you can edit it later.

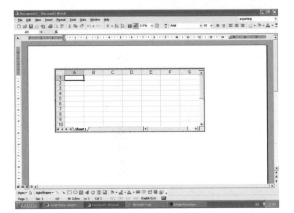

.: Pasting your spreadsheet :.

Then copy and paste your table or data across from one spreadsheet to the new one. Some resizing of the spreadsheet on the page may be required.

PC MASTER TIP

You can edit a spreadsheet in a Word document if you export it correctly.

PROGRESS CHECK EXERCISE

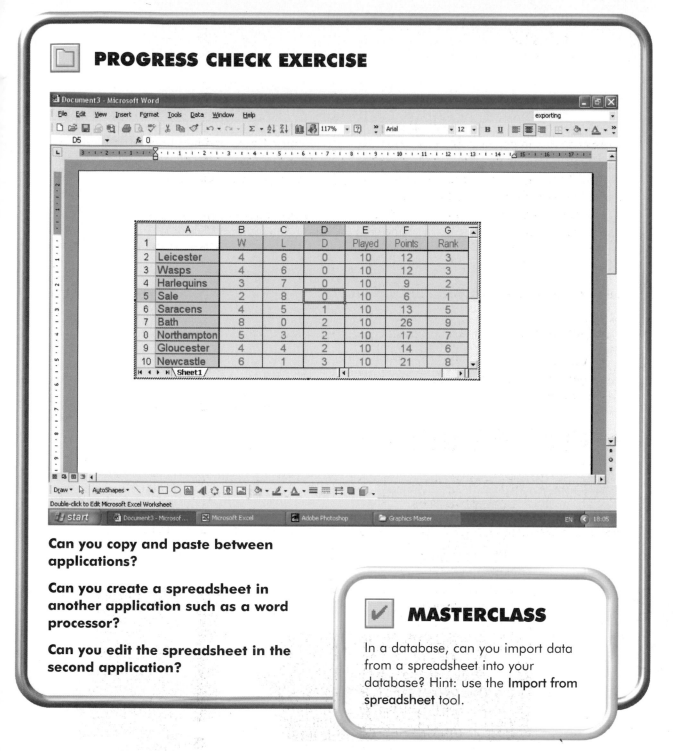

Can you copy and paste between applications?

Can you create a spreadsheet in another application such as a word processor?

Can you edit the spreadsheet in the second application?

✓ MASTERCLASS

In a database, can you import data from a spreadsheet into your database? Hint: use the **Import from spreadsheet** tool.

INDEX